IDEAS, BOMBS, AN

Indian patriots in Lon

CW01508682

Adam Yamey, who is married to an Indian, has been visiting India frequently since 1994. He studied for five years at Highgate School in north London before entering University College London. There, he was awarded a doctorate in physiology, and then qualified as a dental surgeon. After 35 years practising dentistry, he retired. Adam has published books on diverse subjects including, South Africa, the Balkans, India, and Sicily. His most recent book is about travelling in Gujarat.

Front Cover: Replica of India House and statues of Mr and Mrs Shyamji Krishnavarma in Mandvi, Kutch.

ISBN: 978-0-244-20387-0

Published by Adam Yamey with lulu.com

Adam Yamey

IDEAS,

BOMBS,

and

BULLETS

*Indian patriots
in London's Highgate*

The former 'India House' in Highgate today (2019)

"I don't suppose he'd use bombs if he could command a few batteries and half a dozen battalions."
W Somerset Maugham in *Ashenden* (first publ. 1928)

INTRODUCTION

A most unexpected building stands near the seaport of Mandvi in the Kutch district of the State of Gujarat in India. It is a large red brick house with white stone trimmings, typical of Victorian dwellings found in prosperous parts of London. It stands in a flat desert landscape. This structure, which looks brand new, is a replica of a late Victorian residence in the north London suburb of Highgate. Seeing this incongruous building near Mandvi made me curious about the reason for its existence and led me to investigate its story.

This book is about a relatively unknown part of the history of India's struggle for independence from the British. It concerns events centred on Edwardian London. This is a tale of bombs, guns, lawyers, patriots, philosophers, revolutionaries, and scholars.

In the 19th and 20th centuries, before India became independent, many young Indians came to England to be educated. Most of them intended to return to the Indian subcontinent where they could enrich themselves within the constraints imposed by the British, who dominated their country. This volume is about a few Indians, who came to Britain in the first decade of the 20th century, and then, unlike most of their visiting compatriots, risked sacrificing their freedom and prospects of wealth by becoming involved in India's pursuit of freedom.

A tall, large Victorian house stands beside a tree lined residential street in the hilly north London suburb of Highgate. It is this residence that has been replicated in Kutch. Between 1905 and 1910, this house in Highgate, which was then known as 'India House', was a meeting place and hostel for Indian students, many of whom wished to help liberate India from centuries of oppressive British domination.

British imperialism began in India gradually with the arrival in the region of the East India Company in the 17th century. It was consolidated by the British Government in 1858. On the 15th of August 1947, Great Britain relinquished its imperial control of the Indian Subcontinent, and India became a sovereign nation.

Many factors led to the end of British rule in India. Amongst these were growing anti-British sentiments amongst the Indians, which were fuelled by pro-independence nationalists and their leaders. History gives greatest prominence to the non-violent activities of MK Gandhi (the 'Mahatma') and his colleagues. However, there were others, some well-known such as Subhas Chandra Bose and many others lesser known, who advocated a variety of very different means to attain freedom from British rule.

Some Indian nationalist activists carried out their activities abroad, hoping that they would be safe from the prying eyes of the British authorities in India. They worked in places as far afield as Canada, the USA, Japan, France, Germany, and, surprisingly, in Great Britain, home of the imperialist oppressors. TR Sareen wrote in his book *Indian Revolutionary Movement Abroad (1905-21)*:
"The efforts of the Indian revolutionaries to promote the cause of Indian independence from abroad occupies a unique place in the history of India's struggle for freedom."

Some of the Indians working in Edwardian Britain to liberate India from British domination occupy a relatively obscure, almost forgotten part of the history of India's freedom struggle. This book focusses on their work for the country's freedom by examining what occurred in India House in Highgate between the years 1905 and 1910.

The first part of this book discusses the aspirations of most Indian nationalists during the last half of the 19th century and the early years of the next century. Almost all of them had moderate views and hoped that Indians could achieve some degree of self-government *within* the British Empire.

This will be followed by the story of an Indian, Shyamji Krishnavarma, who came at first to study in England, and then later encouraged a new approach to the future of his country. It was an approach, which contrasted dramatically with that of those who were already established leaders in the movements for reform in India. He and his colleagues desired complete independence of India, an existence *outside* the British Empire.

The text that follows the introductory chapters describes the Indian patriots, who congregated in India House, and their often bold and exciting deeds involving books, bombs and bullets. They performed these, often risking their lives, with the aim of freeing India from the British Empire. The book ends with the story of the replicated house in Mandvi.

Note one: *all spellings of Indian names are transliterations of Indian languages into Latin script. Therefore, inconsistencies in the spelling of a person's name are often encountered.*
Note two: *During the 19th and early 20th centuries, British people living in India were known as 'Anglo-Indians'. Today, the term has a quite different meaning.*
Note three: *In this book 'India House' refers to a house in Highgate, but NOT to India House (built 1928-30) in Aldwych, which is currently part of the Indian High Commission.*

THE 'BENEVOLENT' RULER OF INDIA

Readers who are looking forward to the bombs and bullets mentioned in the title of this book are asked to be patient. This chapter describes some of the 'ideas' mentioned in the title and the historical context of India House. Without understanding what preceded the founding of this 'centre of sedition' (as it was called by the police and press) in Highgate, little sense can be made of the exciting things that were inspired by those who lived and met there.

The British conquest of India was met by sporadic resistance to it. Until the late 1850s, it was mainly expressed using violence. Examples of this include the Anglo-Mysore conflicts in the 18th century involving the forces of Hyder Ali and Tipu Sultan[1], the Vellore 'Mutiny' of 1808[2] , and the Anglo-Sikh Wars of the 1840s[3]. Violent opposition to the British culminated in the great Revolt or Rebellion of 1857 (aka: 'The Indian Mutiny' and 'First War of Independence'). After 1857, other approaches to attaining self-government avoiding violent means began to predominate. TR Sareen explains this trend:

"In the post-1858 period, tremendous change took place in the intellectual, economic, and social conditions of the people…"
This was because:
"The spread of the English pattern of education and the impact of ideas of liberty, equality and nationalism provided the motive force for the growth of the national movement…"
The relatively few Indians who benefitted from the British educational system, which offered them a variety of lucrative opportunities, had:
"…an implicit faith in the British sense of justice and fondly hoped that as soon as they proved themselves fit, they would be entrusted a larger share in the administration of their own country. [4]"

The idea that British rule was beneficial to the Subcontinent persisted amongst members of both the British and Indian elites, even after the bloody upheavals in India that began in 1857, which were harshly suppressed by them. The Indian Dadabhai Naoroji, (1825-

1917), a spokesman for India in England and once a Liberal MP in the British House of Commons, wrote:

"Nobody can more appreciate the benefits of the British connexion than I do ... I am most sincerely ready to accord my gratitude for any benefit which Britain can rightly claim.[5]"

Naoroji's sentiments were shared by many in Britain, whether they were Indian or British. It was generally believed in Britain that India was better off being ruled by the British, who considered that they were bringing a 'superior civilisation' to the Subcontinent. The unfortunate belief amongst northern Europeans that they were superior to Africans and Asians was shared by many highly respected 19th century intellectuals including, for example, Thomas Jefferson, Ernst Haeckel, Charles Darwin, Georges Cuvier, and Arthur Schopenhauer[6]. It provided a justification for European imperialism and the 'rape and pillage' of the 'brown' and 'black' peoples.

With few exceptions, scarcely anyone publicly objected to the idea that British rule in India was a 'good thing' for the people of the Subcontinent. One notable objector was Karl Marx (1818-83), a 'father' of socialism. He wrote over thirty articles about India for the *New York Daily Tribune* between 1853 and '58. One of these, which was published on the 25th of June 1853, revealed the effect of British rule, then administered by the British East India Company, on the state of the subcontinent. Marx wrote:

"There cannot, however, remain any doubt but that the misery inflicted by the British on Hindostan is of an essentially different and infinitely more intensive kind than all Hindostan had to suffer before.... England has broken down the entire framework of Indian society, without any symptoms of reconstitution yet appearing. This loss of his old world, with no gain of a new one, imparts a particular kind of melancholy to the present misery of the Hindoo[7], and separates Hindostan, ruled by Britain, from all its ancient traditions, and from the whole of its past history.... England, it is true, in causing a social revolution in Hindostan, was actuated only by the vilest interests, and was stupid in her manner of enforcing them.[8]"

Four years later, a large-scale revolt against the British, the Rebellion, began in early May of 1857. It continued until November of the following year. The outbreak was caused by many factors that ranged from grievances amongst Indian soldiers under the command of the British to wider social discontent. Field Marshal Lord Roberts (1832-1914), who was born in 'British' India and led the British forces to victory during the Second Anglo-Boer War in South Africa, wrote about these social factors:

"... *the revolt, in my judgment, would never have taken place had there not been a feeling of discontent and disquiet throughout that part of the country from which our Hindustani sepoys chiefly came, and had not certain influential people been thoroughly dissatisfied with our system of government...*[9]"

Another writer, Mr James Kennedy, a missionary at Benares, confirmed that Indians were dissatisfied with British rule:

"*What I have heard asserted by scores of individuals is, that our whole system, missions, schools, rail ways, electric telegraphs, etc., is taking away and destroying their religion; they can stand it no longer.*[10]"

Writing in *The New York Daily Tribune* of 17th September 1857, Karl Marx confirmed the existence of non-military causes of the 1857 rebellion:

"... *the British rulers of India are by no means such mild and spotless benefactors of the Indian people as they would have the world believe. For this purpose, we shall resort to the official Blue Books ... on the subject of East-Indian torture, which were laid before the House of Commons during the sessions of 1856 and 1857 ... According to the Report of the Chief Commissioner for the Punjaub, it was proved that:* "... *in matters under ... direction of the Deputy-Commissioner, Mr. Brereton himself, the houses of wealthy, citizens had been causelessly searched; that property seized on such occasions was detained for lengthened periods; that many parties were thrown into prison, and lay there for weeks, without charges being exhibited against them; and that the laws relating to security for bad character had been applied with sweeping and indiscriminating severity...* "[11]"

The Rebellion of 1857/8 was extraordinarily bloody. Many innocent people, both British and Indian, suffered unimaginable cruelties and often death. Eventually, the British restored the subcontinent to a more 'peaceful' state. However, much irreversible damage had been done. The 'victorious' British felt the need to avenge their fellow ('white') men and women, who had become victims of the

Indian rebels. Rather than resorting to the justice system, for which Britain had rightfully attained a good reputation, many Indians were cruelly tortured and killed by British men (aided by some Indians loyal to them) after the uprising was over, often without even the pretence of a judicial hearing. William Dalrymple gives several graphic examples of British cruelty in his book about the period. One example suffices. He wrote of:

"… how every village in the path of the army was torched, and old men, women and children were burned to death in their houses; of how the Sikhs were allowed to torture, impale and burn alive the captured sepoys … But that was not the end: Neill[12] ordered that contrary to the dictates of both faiths, all Hindus were then 'to be buried, and the Mahommedans burned'[13]"

The random vengeance killing by the British of anyone Indian, whether guilty or not of harming 'white' European people during the Revolt and without resort to fair trial, resembled what the Germans perpetrated in WW2. The mass revenge killings of innocent people in places like Lidice in Czechoslovakia and Oradour-sur-Glane in France come to mind. On the 1st of October 1858. Marx wrote perceptively:

"The cruelty of the retribution dealt out by the British troops, goaded on by exaggerated and false reports of the atrocities attributed to the natives … have not created any particular fondness for the victors. On the contrary, … the hereditary hatred against the Christian intruder is more fierce than ever…[14]"

The desire for revenge was strong in England. The journalist and writer George Dodd described how the Earl of Derby urged that England should deal with the 'mutineers' after due judicial process, and then:

" '… For every man taken with arms in his hands there ought to be a righteous punishment, and that punishment death. For those miscreants who have perpetrated unmentionable and unimaginable atrocities upon women, death is too mild a sentence. On them should be inflicted the heavier punishment—a life embittered by corporal punishment in the first instance, and afterwards doomed to the most degrading slavery[15] … Measures should be taken to convince the natives that the English are their masters; but they must also be convinced that the English are their benefactors….'[16]"

The idea expressed by the words such as the Earl's *"the English are their benefactors"* created a misconception in the minds of influential Indians living both in England and India during the 19th and (early) 20th centuries. Many important British people believed that it was really the case that British rule was ultimately beneficial for the future of the Indian subcontinent, but not everyone. For example, the Positivist philosopher Richard Congreve (1818-99), whose ideas greatly influenced the founder of India House in Highgate, disputed the benefits that British domination offered to India. In November 1857, whilst the Rebellion was in full swing, he published a booklet entitled *India*, which proposed that the British should give up its hold on the country. He wrote:

"Besides, the question once forcibly brought home to us [i.e. by the rebellion], *the uneasy consciousness of the weakness of our cause has been aroused from its dormant state. This consciousness betrays itself in the seeking for, and the production of, higher reasons than those which have been in vogue for retaining our hold on India ... We occupied India under the impulse of commercial and political motives; we have governed it as a valuable appendage, commercially and politically. This is the broad truth. When our Empire is tottering to its fall, then to step forward with moral or Christian motives for holding it, which have never influenced our previous policy, is a very questionable course ... I proceed to state the policy which I think it is the duty of England to adopt towards India. It is simple in the extreme. It is, that we withdraw from our occupation of India without any unnecessary delay ..."*

Elsewhere in his booklet, Congreve questions whether the British have a right to govern India to promote 'civilisation':

"The third reason alleged for our retention of India is, the interests of Civilization. It is urged that, released from our hold, she would fall back into disorder and barbarism. I frankly own that such a plea has no weight with me ..."

Congreve's publication also addressed the working people of Britain, whom he felt, probably rightly, received few of the benefits derived by the British occupation of far-off India. He compared the arrogance of the British towards their subjects in the Subcontinent with that of the upper classes in Britain towards the British working people. Then, he asked his British readers to put themselves in the 'shoes of the Indians' to understand how the latter felt about their British occupiers. He asked how the British would have felt had the Normans invaded their country, as the British had invaded India, and then not intermarried and mixed with the English (as the Normans did), but instead had kept themselves separate and asserted their superiority in the same way as the British had done in India. In this theoretical situation, he felt that the British would have tried to prevent their country:

"... from being the victim of foreign oppression... [17]*"*

In 1857, Congreve was almost alone in his public criticism of British domination of India. Many years later, published sentiments like his became more widespread both in India and in Great Britain.

One important result of the outbreak and suppression of the 1857 rebellion was that control over India was taken away from the East India Company (whose ineptitude[18] had been blamed as a primary cause of the Rebellion of 1857) and placed into the hands of the British Government. On the 1st of November 1858, Queen Victoria's *Proclamation to the Princes, Chiefs, and People of India* was read in the principal cities of India. This promised Indians that they would be treated benevolently by their British rulers, as these four quotes from the *Proclamation* suggest:

"We hold ourselves bound to the natives of our Indian territories by the same obligations of duty which bind us to all our other subjects ..."

"...We declare it to be our Royal will and pleasure that none be in anywise favoured, none molested or disquieted, by reason of their religious faith or observances, but that all shall alike enjoy the equal and impartial protection of the law; and we do strictly charge and enjoin all those who may be in authority under us that they abstain from all interference with the religious belief or worship of any of our subjects, on pain of our highest displeasure...."

"...And it is our further will that, so far as may be, our subjects, of whatever race or creed, be freely and impartially admitted to offices in our service, the duties of which they may be qualified, by their education, ability, and integrity, duly to discharge..."

"...When ... internal tranquillity shall be restored, it is our earnest desire to stimulate the peaceful industry of India, to promote works of

public utility and improvement, and to administer its government for the benefit of all our subjects resident therein...[19]"

These were fine words, which Victoria herself, who was well-disposed to India[20], probably believed, but they were rarely translated into deeds. Indian leaders in England and many in India believed in their truth, but they had some reservations. They felt that should a few defects in the way the British governed India be corrected, there was no reason why the words so nobly proclaimed by the Queen could not retain their credibility. However, at least one Indian freedom fighter was not so sure about this. VD Savarkar, one of the chief protagonists in this book, wrote with hindsight:

"This Proclamation of the Queen was just another 'peaceful' device that the British had found out, as they had used the other one of 'violent repression', simply to put down the Indian revolutionaries. They had not the least intention to follow in future the political or administrative policy outlined in it.[21]"

However, many Indian leaders retained their faith in the benevolence of the British. For example, Sir Mancherjee Bhownaggree (1851-1933), a Conservative MP born in India, stated in the House of Commons on the 15th of February 1898:

"The people of India believe the English rule over them to be a beneficent rule...[22]"

And in 1902, Dadabhai Naoroji looked back on his earlier thoughts on the British Empire and his faith in the well-meaning of the British:

"As far as I am concerned I have ever expressed my faith in the British conscience ... That faith, after all the vicissitudes and disappointments which have marked the last half century, I still hold.[23]"

Even MK Gandhi (1869-1948; the 'Mahatma'), who later became famous for his role in the struggle for India's independence from the British, wrote in 1903:

"We want to serve the community, and in our own humble way to serve the Empire. We believe in the righteousness of the cause, which it is our privilege to espouse. We have an abiding faith in the mercy of the Almighty God, and we have firm faith in the British Constitution.[24]"

It is only fair to note that Gandhi's belief in the 'righteousness' of the British was destroyed a few years later, after cruel British actions in

India such as, for example, the Rowlatt Act and the massacre at Jallianwala Bagh in 1919.

Gandhi's early belief in the ultimate beneficence of the British towards India was shared by most of the Indian nationalist organizations in Britain during the 19th century. These included[25]: the London Indian Society (founded 1865), the East India Association (1866), the Indian Constitutional Reform Association (1884), and the better known Indian National Congress (founded in 1885 by the Englishman Allan Octavian Hume[26], Dadabhai Naoroji, and others). The aim of these groups was to increase Indian participation in the government of India and to seek amelioration of conditions in the country. During the 19th century, members of these organizations hoped that reforms could be made to life in India within the framework of the 'civilised' British Empire. Freeing India from British rule was not on their agendas.

During the second half of the 19th century, the more highly educated class of Indians in India and specially in Britain:
"… had an implicit faith in the British sense of justice and fondly hoped that as soon as they proved themselves fit, they would be entrusted with a larger share in the administration of their own country. However, with passing of years they felt disappointed and disillusioned as they found that the despotic rule of an alien power gave them no opportunities and denied them their legitimate role in the regeneration of the national life[27]."
Most of the Indian intelligentsia had studied in the British system of education. They had become prosperous, for example as barristers and civil servants, within the framework of British rule. Those with successful careers in India had much to gain from the maintenance of British domination of the country. This was also the case of those who sought reforms within the boundaries of British rule.

A man from Kutch in western India became an exception to what has just been described. His arrival in London from India in 1897 heralded the establishment within Great Britain of a movement, whose aims were not to improve India under British rule, but to rid the country of its British 'oppressors' by any means. His ideas became the catalyst for the use of bombs and bullets at India House.

THE MAN FROM KUTCH

Shyamji Krishnavarma[28] ('Shyamji') was born in Mandvi, an estuarine seaport in Kutch, in 1857. Until June 1948[29], Kutch, a largely arid desert area, was one of the semi-autonomous Indian Princely States controlled by the British Government in India. Sandwiched between Sindh (now in Pakistan) and the Saurashtra peninsula, Kutch is now part of the State of Gujarat.

Building a dhow in Mandvi

Mandvi was an important trading centre. It was surrounded by a long wall, constructed in the 16th century and now mostly demolished. The old heart of the town and its bustling bazaar area remains picturesque with many houses displaying intricately carved wooden structural and decorative features. One bank of the mouth of the River Rukmavati continues to be a thriving centre for the construction of traditional wooden *dhows*, which are favoured for transporting goods mainly between the Arabian Gulf and East Africa. Fishermen mend their nets and maintain their colourfully decorated small vessels on the opposite bank. Mandvi is probably best known for the Vijay Vilas, a Maharao's palace built in the 1920s in a Rajput architectural style. It was used to film some of the scenes in the highly popular Bollywood movie *Lagaan*, which was released in 2001 and depicts the struugle between the Indians and the British.

Shyamji was born into a poor Bhanasali family. The Bhanasali community comprises mainly poorer farmers and traders, who are Vaishnavite Hindus, worshippers of Vishnu (an avatar of Krishna) [30]. Krishnavarma's first name, Shyamji, can mean: 'dark complexioned', 'dark blue' (as Krishna is often portrayed), and 'Krishna'[31]. It was an obvious choice for a son's name by worshippers of this god. The 'Varma' suffix on his surname was questioned by members of the Indian police in British India, who became very interested in Shyamji's activities after 1905. A police report dated 27th September 1905 suggested Shyamji:

"... *added the title "Varma" to his name in order to pass himself off as a Kshatriya*[32]..."

This might have been a defamatory act of the authorities against someone they feared. If this was really the case, it might have been added because the Kshatriya (warrior) caste is believed to be superior in status to that of the Bhanasali people and some members of Shyamji's family's caste claim to be of Kshatriya descent[33]. Fischer-Tiné wrote that despite his name Shymaji was not a Kshatriya[34]. Regardless of whether he was a Kshatriya, Shyamji's educational successes allowed him to mix with men from backgrounds more prosperous than his.

Young Shyamji attended the local primary school in Mandvi from 1870 onwards[35], and continued his education in the Alfred High School in Bhuj (60 kilometres northeast of Mandvi). The language of tuition in Bhuj was English. He was an excellent student and topped the school in academic achievement. His father, who had a small business in Bombay where he lived, may have given news of Shyamji's prowess to members of a group of reformers based in Bombay[36], with whom he had business relations. Some of them had family members in Kutch, who might have also heard about the child prodigy. In any case, news of Shyamji's scholastic excellence reached the ears of men who were prepared to help bright young Hindu men.

The reformers in Bombay were followers of the Arya Samaj movement (see below). Led by men such as Vishnu Parsaram Shastri,

Madhavdas Raghunathdas, Karsandas Mulji (sometimes called an 'Indian Luther'[37]), and others, the Arya Samaj reformers fought against pillars of Hindu Brahminical tradition such as: untouchability, child marriage, enforced widowhood, sati (widows' self-immolation by burning), and worship of idols. One of these gentlemen, a Bhatia merchant and philanthropist from Kutch called Mathuradas Lavaji[38], paid for Shyamji to enter the Wilson High School in Bombay to continue his studies.

Lavaji was one of several Bombay businessmen who defended[39] Karsandas Mulji (1832-75) during the famous Maharaj Libel Case (1861-62)[40]. Mulji, a journalist, had written in a newspaper, *Satya Prakash*, that Jadunathji Brijratanji, the head of the Vallabhacharya sect of the Vaishnavas, was guilty of practising all kinds of dubious and immoral activities in the name of religion. Mulji won the case. It was an important trial because it encouraged many in Bombay to begin thinking about the immoral and irreligious abyss into which much of Brahminical Hinduism had descended. Lavaji was in sympathy with the reformers of Hinduism in Bombay.

Shyamji was kept busy in Bombay. Not only did he attend classes at Wilson High School, but he also studied Sanskrit in a *paathshala*[41] run by Shastri Viswanath, a Sanskrit teacher who was a hereditary priest in the Kutchi Bhatia community[42]. It was requirement of pupils who, like Shyamji, had received scholarships or financial assistance from the Bombay reformers that they pursue studies in Sanskrit, the language of the Vedas. The Vedas are the earliest Hindu texts, believed to have been transmitted to the Aryans, possibly first inhabitants of India, directly from Heaven[43]. Traditionally under the guardianship of the Brahmins, over the centuries the texts became, it was believed by reformers such as those in Bombay, corrupted or modified to suit the not always worthy purposes of the Brahmins. The reason that the reformers wanted young men like Shyamji to pursue studies in Sanskrit was to help their movement study the 'original' texts of the Vedas, which they believed to be unaffected by later accretions and interpretations that diluted their purity.

As in Bhuj, Shyamji became a first-class student in Bombay. His academic ability and knowledge of Sanskrit won him the Seth Gokuldas

Kahandas Parekh[44] scholarship, which paid for him to study at Elphinstone High School, a much more expensive and prestigious establishment than Wilson High School. His great knowledge of Sanskrit allowed him to use the title 'Pandit[45]'. Elphinstone's pupils were mainly the sons of Bombay's wealthy elite. It was here that Shyamji became a friend of a pupil Ramdas, son of Chhabildas Lallubhai, a wealthy Bhanasali merchant of Bombay. Chhabildas was impressed by Shyamji. He asked Shyamji, then aged eighteen, to marry his daughter Bhanumati with her approval[46] (possibly unusually for the period), then aged thirteen. They married in 1875.

The year before his marriage, Shyamji met Swami Dayanand Saraswati ('Dayanand'; 1824-83), who became important in his life. The Swami had come to Bombay to meet members of the reforming movement, with which Shyamji had become associated.

Dayanand[47] was an influential reformer of Hinduism and the founder of the Arya Samaj movement. He was born in Tankara, which is now in the Morbi district of the State of Gujarat. To escape from a forced marriage in childhood and disillusioned by his family's slavish Hindu devotional practices, he wandered around India as a *sannyasa* (religious mendicant) for well over a decade. During this period, he met and became a disciple of Virajanand Dandeesha (1778-1868), who was a scholar and teacher of Sanskrit and the texts of the Vedas. Dayanand promised Dandeesha that he would devote his life to the renaissance of the Hinduism of the Vedas[48]. Dayanand rejected Hinduism of the Puranas and other later texts and became convinced that the 'pure' Hinduism as found in the Vedas was the only true form of the religion[49]. He wanted to purify Hinduism by stripping away modifications introduced after the texts in the Vedas were received from Heaven[50]. In 1875, Dayanand published his book *Satyarta Prakash* ('Light of Truth')[51], which expounds his beliefs. Banned in some parts of India when it was published, it contains some quite inflammatory material. Dayanand believed that God is the:
"...*eternal source of all knowledge and he reveals it through the Vedas...*[52]",
and that because the Vedas are the sole source of knowledge, all other religions are imperfect. His book contains chapters, which seek to prove that religions apart from pure Hinduism, based solely on the Vedas, are

fatally flawed, and therefore to be avoided. Dayanand's arguments against other religions are based on literal interpretations of selected texts from holy books, such as The Bible and The Koran, without appreciating or admitting that what is written in these texts should not be interpreted literally[53].

According to Dayanand, the arrival of the Aryans into India (now a subject of some contention) marked the start of a 'Golden Age'. He wrote:

"In the 'Golden Days' of India, saints and seers, princes and princesses, kings and queens, and other people used to spend a large amount of time and money in performing and helping others to perform Homa[54]; and so long as this system lasted, India was free from disease and its people were happy.[55]"

This Golden Age had long passed because, putting it simply, Hindus had modified and ignored the teachings in the Vedas. However, he believed:

"It can become so again, it the same system were revised…",

by which he meant if Hinduism were to be reformed and people returned to a strict adherence to the Vedas, the 'Golden Age' would be revived.

Dayanand blamed the decline of India and its subjection by various invaders to the deviation of Hindus and their religious leaders from the practices advocated in the Vedas. He wrote:

"The causes of foreign rule in India are:- mutual feud, differences in religion, want of purity in life, lack of education, child-marriage, marriage in which the contracting parties have no voice in the selection of their life-partners, indulgence in carnal gratification, untruthfulness and other evil habits, the neglect of the study of the Veda, and other mal-practices.[56]"

Dayanand believed that the advances of the Europeans that allowed them to conquer his India was due to their avoidance of things that had contributed to the downfall of Hinduism[57]. The conquerors' successes were in his opinion due to their valuing the following: good education; willingness to sacrifice everything for the good of their nations; not imitating others blindly; obeying superiors; helping their fellow countrymen with trade; and not being . lazy. Absence of these characteristics, which Dayanand believed to be beneficial for the success of the British, contributed, in his opinion, to the downfall of India. Furthermore, deviation from the Vedas added to his impression that India lacked the 'superiority' he detected amongst the British and other Europeans.

In 1875, Dayanand formed the Arya Samaj ('Aryan' 'society'). Its objects were: to promote Dayananda's version of reformed Hinduism (based only on the original, unmodified texts of the Vedas); to counter attacks on Hinduism made by Christians and members of other religions; to convert back to Hinduism those who had been converted to Islam and Christianity; to reinterpret caste by allocating people into a caste according to their merits rather than by accident of birth; and to promote the idea that the Vedas contained the original plans for what were regarded as modern inventions[58]. As an example of the latter, he wrote:

"... *that Krishna and Arjuna went to America in an Ashwatari vessel (i.e., one propelled by electricity) and brought the sage Uddalaka back with them ...*"

The Arya Samaj, in common with the Brahmo Samaj, strove to reform Hinduism, but differed from the Brahmo Samaj in many respects. Members of Arya Samaj had no faith in the goodness of the British Government, whereas the opposite was true for the Brahmo Samaj. Arya Samaj believed in the superiority of Hinduism over other religions, whereas the Brahmo Samaj put Hinduism on the same level as other religions. Another of many differences between the two movements was that Arya Samaj wanted to revive Vedic traditions and to reject modern western culture and philosophy, whereas the Brahmo Samaj accepted western culture and ideas[59].

Many of the religious reformers in Bombay's Gujarati and Kutchi mercantile circles followed Dayanand, as did some future promoters of Indian self-government. The Arya Samaj opened a branch in Bombay, which attracted many of the reformers, including Shyamji's father-in-law, to join it. Many students of Elphinstone College also became members of the organization.

While visiting Bombay, Dayanand met Shyamji, who then received private lessons in Sanskrit from him. Shyamji and Dayanand rapidly became friends and corresponded with each other. Their friendship might have been enhanced by the fact that Dayanand's mother came from Kutch, as had Shyamji[60]. Shyamji provided valuable assistance in the editing and distribution of Dayanand's Vedic publications.

In 1876, a serious eye infection made it difficult for Shyamji to study for the examinations to gain admission to Bombay University[61]. He failed the matriculation examinations, which was a serious blow to him and his backers. The latter, leading members of the reform movement, encouraged him to use his skills to propagate the message of the reformed Hinduism that they were advocating. So, in 1877, Shyamji made a tour of northern and western India, giving lectures on the religious and social reforms inspired by the work of Dayanand and reformers sympathetic to his ideas. He was able to give public lectures in various languages[62] including Sanskrit, Hindi, Gujarati, and English. He was a good orator and his lectures were well received.

The arrival in Bombay of a scholar from Oxford in 1876 was a turning point in Shyamji's life. The scholar was the orientalist Monier Monier-Williams[63] (1819-99), an Englishman who was born in Bombay. He had become Professor of Sanskrit at the University of Oxford in late 1860. In 1876, Monier-Williams had come India to elicit donations from Indian princes to help finance his project to create an institute dedicated to furthering studies of Indian culture at Oxford. His Indian Institute was established in 1883, and finally opened in 1896[64].

During his visit to India in 1876, Monier-Williams wanted to find a man who could read and write Sanskrit in the Devanagari script[65], in which, for example, the Vedas were originally recorded in writing (after having been transmitted from one generation to the next orally and learnt by rote). Judge Gopal Rao Hari Deshmukh (1823-92), a social reformer belonging to the Chitpavan[66] community of Maharashtra, introduced Monier-Williams to Shyamji, the brilliant young scholar of Sanskrit. Incidentally, it was Gopal Rao, who after hearing Shyamji lecture in Nasik in 1877, said:

"I have heard his lectures in Sanskrit, they were very able and correct. He is a very promising youth, very well behaved and good tempered young man.[67]"

Monier-Williams was impressed by Shyamji. The *Times of India*, dated 22nd May 1877 reported:

"A young pandit of Gujarat whose attainments in Sanskrit have been the admiration of his brethren of Nasik and Poona has lately attracted much attention among the Hindu savants. During Prof. Monier Williams' visit to western India, this precocious scholar and reformer attracted Professor's attention and he strongly urged on him the benefits that would accrue to him by paying a visit to England. Among his [Shyamji's] admirers are, Rao Bahadur, Gopalrao Hari Deshmukh, Mahadev Govind Ranade and Ganesh Vasudev Joshi.[68]"

At first, Monier-Williams was unable to entice Shyamji to follow him back to Oxford. Instead of that or reapplying for Bombay University, Shyamji travelled on his lecture tour, already mentioned. However, by 1879, he felt ready to go to Oxford. His biographer Yajnik wrote:

"Oxford seemed to beckon him like a shining star from afar to its ancient portals. Turned down by a youthful University, he would seek admission to one of the oldest seats of learning. Insuperable difficulties stood in the way. His hopes were, however, centred on the great Sanskrit Professor, to whom he could render the most valuable assistance in editing and deciphering Sanskrit texts. All that he needed to do was to deepen the impression of his Sanskrit scholarship on the Professor's mind, and to secure public recognition in India of his outstanding mastery of Sanskrit language and literature.[69]"

This, he was able to do after giving a series of lectures in Nasik in Sanskrit. After giving these discourses in the ancient Indian language, he received written commendations signed by Judge Gopal Rao, then a member of the Arya Samaj in Nasik[70].

Having demonstrated his skills in Sanskrit at Nasik, the young Pandit began looking towards accepting Monier Williams's earlier invitation and attending Oxford. The judge wrote to Monier Williams strongly recommending that Shyamji would make an ideal assistant in his studies of Sanskrit. The professor was delighted at the prospect of having the young Pandit in Oxford. Well-wishers amongst the reformers hoped that Shyamji would return from Oxford to continue his excellent missionary work, promoting reform of Hinduism as envisaged by the Arya Samaj. For example, the leading social reformer and a founding member of the Indian Congress Party, Judge Mahadev Govind Ranade (1842-1901)[71] wrote to Shyamji:

"If you continue your Sanskrit studies and go to Europe, keep before your mind's eye the noble object of devoting your life to the missionary work of the true Vedic faith. Our great want is that of earnest and well-taught missionary agency: we expect you to lead the way. . . Improve your Sanskrit studies, beat the Shastri[72] in his own element, with his own weapons, and be animated by the flame which God alone vouchsafes.[73]"

According to an unflattering police report written in September 1905[74], Shyamji might have sold some of his wife's jewellery to pay for the sea passage to India. Alternatively, he might have borrowed the money from his wife[75]. He was also lent money by Dr and Mrs Gersen De Cunha[76], because the (British) Political Agent in Kutch was opposed to Shyamji being awarded a scholarship by the Kutch State. He appealed unsuccessfully for funds from the reformers amongst the Gujarati merchant community in Bombay[77]. These men were concerned that Shyamji would abandon his study of the sacred knowledge in the Vedas and reform and then pursue a more lucrative career, as did many of the young Indians who went abroad to study. It was not only the Gujarati reformers who feared this, but also Colonel Olcott and Madame Blavatsky[78], leading lights in the Theosophical Society, which at that time considered itself allied to the Arya Samaj. Dayanand, who supported the idea of Shyamji's visit to England at first, also began to have reservations about it.

Shyamji felt he needed to go to England not only because he was tempted by the academic reputation of Oxford, but also because he wanted to fulfil his father-in-law's high expectations of him, for example by becoming a barrister, which had been thwarted by his failure to enter Bombay University. Shyamji travelled to England on the *SS India*. He was admitted to Balliol College, Oxford, in April 1879 and was awarded a BA in 1882[79].

Despite the financial assistance he had received before leaving India, Shyamji was very short of money in England. Monier Williams paid him a modest weekly stipend, but this was not enough, especially after he had paid his fees to be admitted to study for the Bar Examinations at the Inner Temple in London. After a while, Monier Williams persuaded the British authorities in Kutch to allow him an annual state scholarship of £100 for three years[80].

Shyamji's achievements in Sanskrit were outstanding. His reputation attracted more students to study the language at Oxford, and they paid him for private tutorials. In addition to studying for his BA, he became Monier-William's assistant in Sanskrit studies. Shyamji helped the professor set up his Institute of Sanskrit Studies. He was so highly regarded that in 1881 the Secretary of State selected Shyamji to be an Indian delegate at the 5th International Congress of Orientalists held in Berlin. On the 19th of July 1881, Shyamji delivered a lecture to the Congress. Its subject was *On the importance of Sanskrit as a living language in India*[81]. It was well-received. In addition, he demonstrated his skills in Sanskrit by illustrating:
"*...the subject of Prof. Monier-Williams's paper on the Sandhyd and Brahma-yajna ceremony of the Brahmans by the performance of the sacred rites and recitation of the Gayatri.*[82]"
Two years later, he gave another paper at the 6th Congress of Orientalists held at Leiden (Holland). His subject was *The Use of writing in Ancient India*[83]. By then, Shyamji had already been awarded his BA degree. He was highly regarded by all the leading indologists of the age in England including the famous German born Professor Max Mueller[84]. So great were Shyamji's achievements in his field of specialisation that in 1882 he was elected a member of the prestigious Empire Club, many of whose members were retired British colonial officials who had worked in India.

In addition to his valuable work on Sanskrit, Shyamji excelled in his studies of: logic, law, political economy, Greek, Latin, the works of Sir Francis Bacon, and other subjects. When Shyamji was awarded his BA degree, Professor Monier Williams wrote of him:
"*Here in Oxford, Pandit Shyamaji, without giving up one iota of his Sanskrit learning, has opened his mind freely to the reception of all the higher forms of European culture. He was quite unacquainted with Greek and Latin when he arrived in England, and yet passed his first examination with great credit after little more than a year's study. At his second examination (Moderations) he attained the requisite*

standard in Logic as well as Greek and Latin; and in the final schools, before taking his degree in B.A. he passed a highly creditable examination in Law, Political Economy, and Bacon's works....

I can certify that Pandit Shyamaji is conversant with the best known works of Sanskrit literature, that he is profoundly acquainted with the best native grammars, and that he knows the great grammar of Panini by heart. Assuredly no English or European teacher could possibly be his equal in expounding the grammar of Indian languages according to the principles of native grammarians. I may add that I know no other Pandit who combines a considerable knowledge of Greek and Latin with great Sanskrit attainments.[85]"

In 1881, following the delivery of a paper, *The Origin of Writing in India*, to the Royal Asiatic Society of London, he was elected a non-resident member of this prestigious organization. As a member of the Inner Temple, he was called to the Bar and became a barrister on November the 17th 1884[86].   Other Indians who qualified at Inner Temple (after he did) include Mahatma Gandhi, Jawaharlal Nehru, and Mohammad Ali Jinnah[87].

Detail of the exterior of the Indian Institute in Oxford

Apart from furthering Sanskrit studies and disseminating his considerable knowledge of the subject, Shyamji interested himself in the works and activities of people in England, who, like him, expressed a hope for justice for Indians living in British-dominated India. One of them, whose ideas attracted him greatly, was Herbert Spencer (1820-1903). Apart from being a philosopher, Spencer was also a biologist, political theorist, sociologist, and anthropologist. He was a life-long opponent of imperialism and Britain's policies on India[88]. Spencer was a strong advocate of:

"... laissez-faire, individualism, natural rights, and capitalism. His call for the limitation of state power was so extensive that it included an individual's right to 'ignore the state'...[89]"

Spencer, a highly original thinker, had:

"... a great interest in whether the state should provide for the poor or whether it was right to colonize India...[90] "

In his one of his last publications, Spencer wrote of imperialism as follows:

""You shall submit! We are masters and we will make you acknowledge it!" These words express the sentiment which sways the British nation in its dealings with the Boer republics; and this sentiment it is which, definitely displayed in this case, pervades indefinitely the political feeling now manifesting itself as Imperialism ... So long as the passion for mastery overrides all others the slavery that goes along with Imperialism will be tolerated ... Among men who do not pride themselves on the possession of purely human traits, but on the possession of traits which they have in common with brutes, and in whose mouths "bull-dog courage" is equivalent to manhood – among people who take their point of honour from the prize-ring, in which the combatant submits to pain, injury, and risk of death, in the determination to prove himself "the better man," no deterrent considerations like the above will have any weight. So long as they continue to conquer other peoples and to hold them in subjection, they will readily merge their personal liberties in the power of the State, and hereafter as heretofore accept the slavery that goes along with Imperialism.[91]"

Shyamji wrote (in 1909) that Spencer was:

"...the scholar with the generous heart, who understood India and pitied it. Nearly all of my arguments are based on his works. His spirit guides me.[92]"

Other men whose works expressed opposition to Britain's injustices in India included the Positivist[93] philosophers like ES Beesly (1831-1915) and SH Swinny (1857-1923), and the socialist HM Hyndman (1842-1921). Shyamji associated with these men[94] as well as with Spencer. Beesly resented the fact that Britain had kept India by the sword and not with the consent of its people[95]. In a speech given in 1864, he said:

"England wrongfully held possession of Gibraltar from Spain, and her conduct in China, Japan, India and elsewhere was cowardly and unprincipled. He urged upon all present to divest themselves of those selfish feelings disguised under the name of patriotism, and to maintain only those principles which their consciences told them were right and just.[96]"

Swinny was in correspondence with nationalists in India (including BG Tilak). According to Gary Peatling:

"Swinny's sympathy for subject peoples' nationalisms led him to join other radicals in a series of conferences and pressure groups seeking to raise awareness of the plight of subject peoples of empires all over the world. Like his Positivist colleagues, he was energetic in exposing the hypocrisy of British commentators who were keen to condemn foreign imperial powers such as the Ottoman empire without criticising Britain's own imperial policy. India was a special interest: As he proudly stated in one speech, India 'next to my own country has the first place in my affections'. [97]"

Hyndman, a promoter of the works of Karl Marx, wrote a book about the woeful state of India, which was published in 1886. A few quotes will illustrate his thoughts about India. The point of his volume was to direct:

"… public attention to the irremediable mischief which must be done in India by a continuance of our present system."

About the frequent famines that afflicted Victorian India, he wrote:

"Famines have proved conclusively that the gravest poverty exists in almost every district. During the twenty years dealt with they were very numerous, and the plan which is now adopted, of making the poorer classes of one province pay to keep alive the mass of the famine-stricken people in another, this process being reversed when the former suffer in turn cannot fail in the end to bring about a terrible catastrophe."

As for the so-called benefits of British rule, he wrote:

"It is useless to argue that a Government is doing well for a people who are suffering, as the natives of India have been suffering, under our rule."

On the draining of India's wealth and economic distress, about which much of Hyndman's book is concerned, he wrote:

"The truth is that Indian society, as a whole, has been frightfully impoverished under our rule, and that the process is going on now at an increasingly rapid rate."

Hyndman suggested that India would fare better if it were ruled by its own people and that many of the British should leave:

"To say that in future India must be governed for the sake of its inhabitants, means undoubtedly the displacement in the future of most of our own countrymen from offices in that country."

And, also, he wrote that if the British (i.e. 'we' in this quote):

"... cannot keep India save by inflicting perpetual impoverishment and starvation upon an increasing number of the population, then we cannot leave the country too soon. [98]*"*

In an article published in 1911, Hyndman expounded his long-held belief:

"... how impossible it is that our hold upon India should be permanent."

And he concluded:

"Let us lift off this carapace of greed and repression and hold out the hand of welcome and encouragement to the higher aspirations of this vast population. That England should herself take the first steps towards the complete emancipation of India would entitle her to an infinitely higher place in the world's esteem than a vain attempt to carry on for yet a few fatal years the harmful despotism of to-day. [99]*"*

Having been turned down (inexplicably) as a candidate for a professorship in Sanskrit at London's University College[100] and not been offered a teaching position at Oxford, Shyamji decided to return to India. With the ideas of the people described above and those of Richard Congreve (see the previous chapter) ringing his mind, and bearing flattering testimonials from many important men, Shyamji and his wife[101] returned to India in January 1885. He carried with him a glowing recommendation written by Lord Northbrook, a former Viceroy of India and a fellow member of the Empire Club. It certified that Shyamji was well-qualified to hold a high post in Government service[102].

THE ROVING DIWAN

This chapter provides some information about Shyamji Krishnavarma's life in India after he returned from England in 1885. It helps to understand the stance he was to take regarding the British Empire.

On the 19th January 1885, Shyamji was enrolled as an advocate at the High Court of Bombay[103]. This could have marked the beginning of a lucrative career for him and, also, a stepping-stone to a senior position in the British Government of India. But this was not to be, as an opportunity arose for him to take a senior post in one of the Princely States.

During the British occupation of India, the subcontinent was divided up into areas directly under British rule and others, the Princely States, which were governed by nominally independent rulers, members of local royal families. The rulers of these states were supervised by British-appointed officials such as 'Political Agents' and their subordinates. How the rulers treated their people was of little concern to the British, provided that the states maintained their loyalty to the Empire. A ruler of a Princely State risked being replaced by another member of his royal house if he did anything that was regarded as being against the interests of the British and their maintenance of power in India.

Shyamji and his mentor in India, Dayanand, who was already dead by the time Shyamji returned to India, believed that India could only be freed from British domination if the rulers of the Princely States and their (sometimes large) armies could be encouraged to overthrow the invaders[104]. On his return to India, with that idea in mind, Shyamji thought it would be a good idea to join the governmental services of Princely States rather than those of the British Government in India. And, Indian princes were happy to employ someone with a background as brilliant as his.

His first position was as Diwan (prime minister) of Ratlam, a Princely State founded in 1652 (in what is now Madhya Pradesh). He was appointed on the recommendation of the retiring incumbent, the reformist Gopalrao Hari Deshmukh, who had admired Shyamji's lecturing some years earlier. Shyamji held this position from February[105] (or November[106]) 1886 until 1888, when ill-health forced him to retire prematurely. When Shyamji ended his duty as Diwan, the Rajah of Ratlam gave him a huge leaving bonus[107] in addition to his salary. With this money, Shyamji established three cotton factories at Beawar, Nasirabad, and Kakri, all near Ajmer (in Rajasthan). Also, he began practising as a barrister in Ajmer.

During his time in Ajmer, Shyamji organised a large public protest against the passing of the Age of Consent Bill (which was passed in 1891)[108]. This law raised the age of consent for sexual intercourse from 10 to 12 years for all girls, whatever their marital status. Shyamji was opposed to this new law for several reasons. It hit at Hindu tradition. It went against the spirit of Queen Victoria's proclamation made in 1858. His protest was inspired more by Spencer's beliefs in the rights of individuals[109] than by Arya Samaj.

In April 1893[110], Shyamji was appointed a Member of Council in Udaipur (Mewar State, now in Rajasthan). One of its rulers, Maharana Sajjan Singh (1859-1884), had been a devotee[111] of Shyamji's mentor Swami Dayanand. Dayanand had persuaded him to make reforms including the introduction of Hindi as the language of his state. Dayanand revised his well-known book *Satyarth Prakash* in Udaipur between 1882 and '83[112]. It was under the Maharana Fateh Singh (1849-1930), successor to Sajjan Singh, that Shyamji served the State of Mewar. With the agreement of senior British officials, Shyamji assumed the role of Diwan. As Diwan, he managed to reduce interference by the British in the running of Mewar State, which suited Fateh Singh who was worried that the British were plotting to overthrow him[113]. He need not have worried because he reigned for a long while, from 1884 until 1930, when he died of natural causes.

In 1895, Shyamji was offered the post of Diwan in the Gujarati Princely State of Junagadh. The salary was far greater than what he was getting in Udaipur[114]. Fateh Singh was happy to release him with one year's paid leave and the opportunity to return to his position in Mewar whenever he wished[115].

The move to Junagadh proved disastrous. It soon became evident to Shyamji that the Nawab of Junagadh, Sir Muhammad Rasul Khanji Babi (reigned 1892-1911), took little interest in the running of his state. According to a sycophantic history of the rulers of Junagadh:

"In 1895 A. D. Haridas retired from the post of Diwan. A Barrister named Shyamji Krishna Varma was appointed to succeed him. But as he was found unequal to the work he was removed ...[116]*"*

However, the situation was not as simple as that. Real power in Junagadh was in the hands of a group of men led by the high-ranking Wazir Jamadar Bahuddin, who assumed the duties of Nawab with the latter's agreement. Another official, Mr Puroshottam Rai, whom Shyamji's predecessor allowed to assume the duties of the Diwan, worked together with the Wazir to make decisions on behalf of the Nawab. Shyamji was unhappy working in a state where his subordinate, the Wazir, tried to control his actions as Diwan. Shyamji realised that there was much nepotism and corruption within the Government of Junagadh. When he began to try to do something about this, many officials, who were benefitting from the unsatisfactory situation, became hostile to him. They cooperated with the British authorities to have him summarily dismissed from his position in Junagadh. Shyamji's biographer Yagnik wrote:

"Fate for the first time frowned on him. Here for the first time was he compelled to drink the bitter cup of sorrow and humiliation to its very dregs. The net of State intrigues which he had so successfully escaped up till then closed round him and held him tight in its deadly grip. Then again the British officials and the Agency, who had beamed on him before, suddenly assumed menacing airs and threatening looks. Till at last the impotent Nawab, his intriguing hirelings, and quick-change British officials, all combined to hound him out of Junagadh at twenty-four hours' notice within the extraordinarily short period of less than eight months.[117]*"*

To add insult to injury, not only did Shyamji have to leave without receiving payments due to him but also he was asked to apologise for his 'misdemeanours' to both the Court of Junagadh and the British Political Agent. He refused to give any apologies[118].

The British Agent in Junagadh decided that Shyamji was a "dangerous person" and suggested that the British Residents in all Princely States should be warned against employing him[119]. Alone, this must have been hurtful to Shyamji, but knowing that a former friend at Oxford University, Maconochie, had turned against him must have rubbed salt in the wound.

During his brief stay in Junagadh, Shyamji had helped his former fellow student at Oxford, AF Maconochie of the Bombay Civil Service, to obtain a posting in Junagadh. This offered the Englishman a far higher salary than he had received when working for the British Indian Civil Service. While on his honeymoon and prior to his arrival in Junagadh, Maconochie asked his friend Shyamji to build a home for him and his bride in the state. After Maconochie arrived in Junagadh:

" … *he presently became the rallying centre of all the intrigues brewing against Shyamaji for months past*…[120]"

After benefitting from Shyamji's kindness, not only did Maconochie conspire to get him removed from the government post in Junagadh and have his name blackened amongst the high level British colonial officials in India, but he also shattered Shyamji's belief in the possibility of true friendship between British and Indian people[121].

Having ended his employment at Junagadh prematurely, Shyamji tried to return to his former position in Udaipur. The Maharana was extremely keen to have him back and reinstated him instantly. However, this decision was countermanded by the British Resident in Mewar, WH Curzon Wyllie (1848-1909[122]). On the 8th October 1885, Curzon Wyllie wrote to Shyamji:

"*I should be pleased to see you return to Udaipur were it not that I am told on good authority that you have been dismissed from the Dewanship of Junagadh for misconduct by H.H. the Nabab with the concurrence of the Political Agent in Kathiawar. In these circumstances I regret that I cannot accede to H.H. the Maharana's wish that you should resume business relations with me on the former footing until you have cleared yourself of the imputation which rests on your character and which you assure me is unreserved.[123]"*

The newspapers tried blackening Shyamji's name. Such was the poisoning of Shyamji's reputation by his old 'friend' from Oxford, whom he had helped so recently. However, the Maharana was strong-willed. He insisted on retaining Shyamji as Diwan. Curzon Wyllie had to change his mind and accept Shyamji, but on the condition that he kept:

"... *his name and his new office out of the newspapers for some time.*[124]"

Shyamji decided to sue the Durbar (i.e. court) of Junagadh for unpaid salary due to him. This would have been a large amount because one of the conditions of his employment was:

"...*in the event of the State dispensing with the services of the said Pandit* [Shyamji] *before the expiration of three years the salary for the unexpired period will be paid to him.*[125]"

He appealed to senior British administrators obtain this money, but even those, whom he believed might have supported his case, conspired behind his back to let him down. In mid-1897[126] by which time there was no hope of him receiving any money from Junagadh, Shyamji resigned his lucrative post at Udaipur and soon after that decided to return to England. He realised:

"...*for the first time, the gruesome depth of the vast abyss that separated him and millions of his people, from the handful of Englishmen ruling over his land. ... His faith in Englishmen, individually or collectively, was shattered to smithereens.*[127]"

During his struggle with the British over the Junagadh business during 1896, Shyamji corresponded with the lawyer Bal Gangadhar ('Lokmanya') Tilak (1856-1920). Tilak was by that time a radical member of the Indian National Congress, supporting *swaraj* (self-government) rather than simply an increase in Indian involvement in the governing of British India. He asked Shyamji to send him the papers connected with his dispute with Junagadh. He sent them in order that Tilak could give wider publicity to his case[128]. Shyamji began taking an ever-increasing interest in Tilak's nationalist ideas, which differed radically from the pro-British ideas of the 'moderate' members of the Indian Nationalist Congress[129].

Tilak was a member of the Chitpavan Brahmin caste of coastal Maharashtra. This caste became a prominent community in India following Shivaji's liberation of parts of Maharashtra from Moghul rule in the fourth quarter of the 17th century. Shivaji's descendants were not able to rule the Maratha empire, and control fell into the hands of the Chitpavan chief administrators (*'peshwas'*) until the British defeated the Marathas in 1817. There have been many notable members of the caste, who have made their mark on Indian history. In addition to Tilak, two other Chitpavans, Chiplunkar and Gokhale, played major roles in the early stirrings of the Indian nationalist movement. VD Savarkar, whom we will encounter often in this book, was another Chitpavan who played a significant role in both the independence movement and whose ideas have influenced the political scene in independent India. Contact with Tilak was amongst the reasons that helped Shyamji to choose to depart for England.

It was not for material reasons that Shyamji decided to leave India for London in 1897 because by then:

"He had now reached the comparatively ripe age of 40. With the regular income derived from the three cotton factories in and around Ajmer he was a man of independent means ... he had hastened ... to find ready shelter and solace in the Udaipur State. Nay more. He had even improved his worldly prospects by earning Rs. 2,000 a month instead of Rs. 1,500 he drew in Junagadh.[130]"

His decision to leave India was precipitated by a species of microbe. In September 1896, the first case of bubonic plague was detected in a house in Bombay[131]. It marked the beginning of a huge outbreak of the disease throughout Bombay and its surroundings and Pune (Poona). As part of an attempt to deal with the plague a law, The Epidemic Diseases Act of 1897[132], was enacted by the British on the 4th of February 1897. Measures that were likely to have little or no effectiveness in controlling the disease were inflicted by the British authorities on Indian citizens with viciousness and total disregard for human dignity. Men and women were subjected to whole body examinations, often in public; ships were quarantined; and pilgrims were forbidden to travel. Even corpses were treated with disrespect: before they could be buried or cremated, they were autopsied, a practice that offended both Muslims and Hindus[133].

In March 1897, Shyamji was travelling on a train through Ratlam when it was stopped by British officials, who wanted to examine the passengers to find plague sufferers. He and the other Indian passengers were asked to disembark, and then were treated insultingly in a racist manner. He objected, saying that it was unreasonable that as a traveller in a first-class compartment, he was asked to get out of the train whilst a 'white' European in a second-class carriage was left alone[134].

Soon, the draconian (and useless) actions resulting from the Epidemic Diseases Act, led to civil unrest amongst the Indians. On June the 22nd 1897, Queen Victoria's Diamond Jubilee Day, Walter Rand, the British Head of Plague Control in the Bombay Presidency, a much-hated man, was shot dead along with Lieutenant CE Ayerst, who happened to be with him[135]. They were shot with pistols held by the Chapekar brothers[136], Damodar Hari and Balkrishna Hari, who were Chitpavan Brahmins. They were both hanged.

Many were arrested and imprisoned, often on the flimsiest of grounds, following the Rand assassination. These included BG Tilak, who was accused of writing seditious articles justifying the killing[137], and the Natu brothers of Pune, who were accused of protesting against the atrocious methods the British were employing to combat the plague.

At this point, Shyamji began to worry that things might go badly for him in India and that he risked arrest. For a start, he had been in correspondence with Tilak, who was described by Valentine Chirol, Foreign Editor of the London *Times* (from 1899) as "... *one of the most dangerous pioneers of disaffection*.[138]". Then, there is also a possibility that Tilak might have asked Shyamji to smuggle Damodar Hari Chapekar into one of the armies of a Princely State in order to stir up rebellion[139]. Also, Damodar, who had been known to Tilak for some years before Rand was shot, had been recommended by Tilak to Shyamji for employment as a bodyguard in the service of the Nawab of Junagadh[140]. Given all of these potentially dangerous connections with Tilak and Damodar Chapekar, Shyamji decided that it would be best for him to leave India before he was arrested. Disillusioned with the British, he decided he would fight against their occupation of India from abroad, in a country where he believed freedom of speech and political activities was assured. England was such a place, as he had discovered while he was at Oxford.

LONDON AGAIN

When Shyamji arrived in London, he first resided in rooms provided by the Inner Temple at 13 Kings Bench Walk[141]. During his three year stay there, he amassed a big library that included the works of Herbert Spencer[142]. He hosted many meetings with visiting leading Indian intellectuals, some with nationalist views. During his residence at Inner Temple, the Second Anglo-Boer War (1899-1902) broke out. In far off South Africa, MK Gandhi, the future Mahatma, assisted the British forces. In Shyamji's home in London, the war gave rise to lively discussions. There was considerable opposition to the war in the UK:

"The minority parties and papers, the liberals and the democrats launched an open campaign in the press and on the platform to champion the just cause of the valiant Boers. And Shyamaji being already associated with all such opposition groups easily perceived the truth of the matter from the international standpoint, and denounced the role played by Gandhiji and his Indian followers...[143]"

This war along with his extended studies of Spencer and others helped Shyamji to develop his ideas on the way forward for India.

Although Shyamji came to London as quite a wealthy man and probably invested his money wisely, there is a report that he also made a fortune in the egg business[144]. In 1900, he bought a substantial three storey house opposite Highgate Woods at 9 Queenswood Avenue (now, 60 Muswell Hill Road)[145]. Bought for £880, Shyamji and his wife lived there from the 18th of June 1900 until 1907[146].

At first, Shyamji led a life outside the public eye[147], meeting Indians and others to discuss political matters, often at his new home. In 1899, he made a rare public appearance when he attended the funeral of his Oxford teacher Monier Williams [148], who had died on the 11th of April 1899 in a hotel in Cannes[149], France. His funeral took place in Chessington, Surrey on the 18th April. Shyamji, referred to as "Pundit Shyamaji Krishna Varma" was listed in the *Times* report of the occasion[150]

Krishnavarma's former home opposite Highgate Woods (in 2019)

Shyamji, who had been introduced to rationalism in the writing of the Positivist Herbert Spencer by Dayanand in India, began formulating his attack on the oppressiveness of British rule in India. By 1903, he was ready to show Spencer his scheme for popularising freedom and rationalism[151], but the philosopher died before he could study it.

On the 8th of December 1903, one of the greatest influencer's of Shyamji's philosophy and actions, Herbert Spencer, died at his home in Brighton[152]. On the following day, the *Times* (of London) reported:

"With the death of Herbert Spencer passes away the last and one of the greatest members of the brilliant group which must make the Victorian Age memorable in the history of literature and thought… By those who realized the vastness of his conceptions, he has been compared with Aristotle, sometimes to Hegel, sometimes to Comte; and certainly there is more than a superficial likeness between him and the first of these thinkers in the range and amplitude of their investigation…"

Shyamji attended this highly praised philosopher's cremation at Golders Green Crematorium, which was opened for use about a year before Spencer died. Amongst the mourners at this north-west London funeral were many well-known figures such as, to mention but a few: the scientist Francis Galton; the socialist social reformers and founders of the London School of Economics, Sidney and Beatrice Webb; James Dewar, chemist and inventor of the vacuum flask; the radical English politician Leonard Courtney; and Thomas Hall Caine, playwright and author of a banned drama called *Mahomet* (1890)[153].

As the funeral drew to its close, Shyamji, who was relatively unknown compared with most of the other mourners, made an announcement to those assembled. It marked the beginning of his fame as a public figure. He said:

"After the touching and eloquent oration we have just heard, I hope a few words from a native of India will not be regarded as out of place. The name of Mr. Herbert Spencer is a household word among my educated countrymen. Personally I owe a deep debt of gratitude to the writings of that truly great and good man whose loss we bemoan today. As a trifling token of my respect and esteem I offer £1000 to the memory of the great benefactor of mankind and propose to write to the Chancellor of the ancient and renowned University of Oxford offering the amount for establishing a lectureship to be called the Spencer Lectureship ...[154]*"*

This generous donation thrust Shyamji into the public eye. That he was able to afford it as well as his far from modest home opposite Highgate Woods and other substantial monetary gifts (see below), shows that he was very secure financially. Apart from his egg business, he was also receiving income from his remaining cotton mill (he had sold two of them) in India as well as from prudent investments in the stock exchanges of London, Paris, and Geneva[155].

Oxford University accepted Shyamji's generous gift, which helped to pay for a series of annual Herbert Spencer lectures. The first of these was delivered on the 9th of March 1905[156] by the Positivist philosopher Frederic Harrison, a fellow of Wadham College, who was not only a disciple of Spencer but also of Richard Congreve.

THE YEAR 1905

In 1905, Lord Curzon, Viceroy of India, partitioned Bengal into eastern (mainly Muslim) and western (mainly Hindu) parts. A reason given was to improve administration of the region, but the real reasons were to damage the growing nationalistic activities of the Bengalis and to foment distrust between the Muslims and the Hindus[157]. One of Curzon's biographers wrote:

"The outcry, Curzon predicted, would be loud and fierce in the capital ... but it would not last. As a 'native gentleman' had told him, Bengalis 'always howl until a thing is settled; then they accept it'[158]*"*

But they did not accept it. It was very unpopular in Bengal and all over India. Curzon's policy of 'divide and rule' did much to provoke anti-British sentiments and activities in India. Around this time, protestors against British rule adopted the song *Bande Mataram*[159] (sometimes written as '*Vande Mataram*'), meaning 'Mother, I bow to thee', as their anthem and its name as a patriotic slogan. Shyamji, in London, was inflamed by Curzon's detested deed.

Far away from India, an event occurred. It provided a ray of hope for foreign-dominated people in India and other parts of Asia. On the 5th of September 1905, the Treaty of Portsmouth was signed. Tiny Japan had defeated mighty Russia after a war that began in February 1904[160]. The Japanese victory over a powerful imperialist power gave people in Asia reason to believe that European powers, such as Britain, were not insuperable. And in Russia, the common people rebelled against their Czarist oppressors, a dress rehearsal for the great revolution of 1917. At the same time, other empires such as Ottoman Turkey and China were becoming unsettled.

Events such as these during the year 1905 spurred the wealthy, world-renowned scholar of Sanskrit and former Diwan into political activity that was to have repercussions both in Europe and India. In this momentous year, Shyamji did several significant things to advance the struggle for India's Independence. In January 1905, he published the first issue of his new monthly newspaper *The Indian Sociologist*. Despite its curious name, it was:

"An organ of Freedom and of Political, Social and Religious Reform[161]*"*

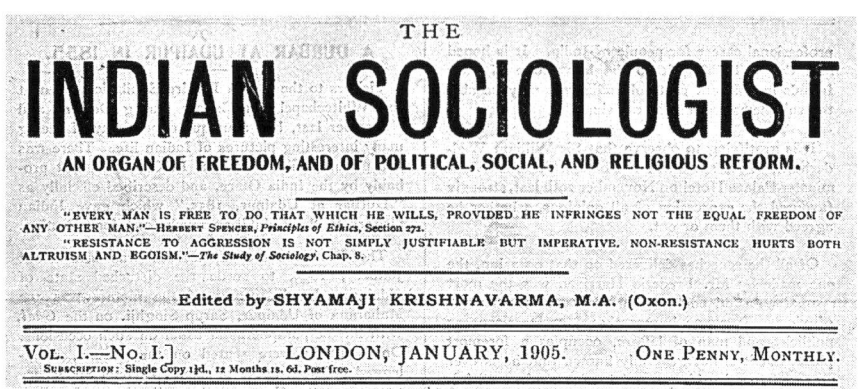

THE

INDIAN SOCIOLOGIST

AN ORGAN OF FREEDOM, AND OF POLITICAL, SOCIAL, AND RELIGIOUS REFORM.

"EVERY MAN IS FREE TO DO THAT WHICH HE WILLS, PROVIDED HE INFRINGES NOT THE EQUAL FREEDOM OF ANY OTHER MAN."—Herbert Spencer, *Principles of Ethics*, Section 272.
"RESISTANCE TO AGGRESSION IS NOT SIMPLY JUSTIFIABLE BUT IMPERATIVE. NON-RESISTANCE HURTS BOTH ALTRUISM AND EGOISM."—*The Study of Sociology*, Chap. 8.

Edited by SHYAMAJI KRISHNAVARMA, M.A. (Oxon.)

VOL. I.—No. I.]   LONDON, JANUARY, 1905.   One Penny, Monthly.
Subscription: Single Copy 1½d., 12 Months 1s. 6d. Post free.

Every issue of the Indian Sociologist *carried these quotes by Herbert Spencer*

His new monthly was to counter what was written in a weekly paper called *India*, which was associated with both the British Committee of the Indian National Congress and The London India Society. These two organizations, which were run by 'moderates' and included British Civil Servants, had no desire to see India detached from the British Empire. In the first issue of *Indian Sociologist*:

"Having implicitly debunked the British "friends" allied to the Indian Congress, Shyamaji proceeded to refer to the genuine and disinterested champions of India's freedom.[162]*"*

These "disinterested champions" included: The Positivist Frederic Harrison; Professor ES Beesly; and Mr SH Swinny. Shyamji described these three as being:

"… among the best friends India has in this country."

In the opening issue, Shyamji reserves his greatest praise for the socialist HM Hyndman:

"Among the friends of India in England must be gratefully remembered the name of Mr. H. M. Hyndman ... who ever since 1873 has persistently pleaded the cause of that unfortunate country, both privately and on public platforms. His numerous articles and papers on such subjects as 'Indian Policy and British Justice' 'Bankruptcy of

India,' etc., have justly entitled him to the gratitude of India. . . He does not believe in half measures, and maintains that the Indians must learn to rely upon themselves, and organise themselves apart from their foreign masters for their final emancipation.[163]"

And, it was the organising of Indians to fight for themselves, as Hyndman proposed, that Shyamji proceeded to do, starting with the publication of *Indian Sociologist*.

In addition to establishing his newspaper, in February 1905 Shyamji also created the 'India Home Rule Society' on the 18th of that month at a meeting held in his home opposite Highgate Woods[164]. The choice of the words 'Home Rule' was inspired by Shyamji's knowledge of the advocates of Irish Home Rule[165]. Amongst those attending the meeting were[166]: Dr C Muthu, Dr DE Pereira, Mr Parmeshwar-Wardy, Mr JC Mukherjee (elected Secretary), and MR Jayakar[167]. Shyamji was elected the President and the vice-presidents were: Mr Parikh, Mr Rana, Mr B Godrej[168], Mr Suhrawardy, and others. Mukherjee was an elderly Bengali, who wrote pieces for Gandhi's *Indian Opinion* as the paper's London correspondent. After joining Shyamji, he continued writing in the same paper, but in his pieces he began adopting a tougher approach than before. For example, he wrote in one issue: "*... crush the white foe, drive out the white foreigner.[169]"* This harsh tone upset Gandhi.

Shyamji wrote about the Society in the second issue of *Indian Sociologist*:

"... a new Pro-Indian organisation has been formed in London under the title of "The Indian Home Rule Society." Thus the prophecy made years ago. by the late Marquis of Salisbury, who while opposing Home Rule for Ireland contended that the proposal to grant Home Rule to Ireland would be followed by a demand for a similar concession to India, has been verified ..."

Next, he criticised the already existing Indian groups in England:

"The present organisations in the United Kingdom, connected with India, are practically all at the disposal of the bureaucrats (Wedderburn, Cotton and Company). It is therefore a matter of paramount importance that a new organisation on independent lines should be set on foot, for obtaining for India what is its indefensible right, 'a Government of the people, by the people, and for the people[170]'
"

Another of the aims of the Society was to send *deshbhaktas* to India. These patriotic missionaries were to preach passive resistance against the colonial British. By 'passive resistance' Shyamji's followers meant:

"*...that Indians can obtain emancipation by simply refusing to help their foreign master without incurring the evils of violent revolution...*[171]"

In other words, if every Indian refused to buy or sell from the British and refused to work in any way on behalf of them, the imperialists would be unable to exist in India. This rather optimistic plan antedated a similar idea carried out on a much larger scale by MK Gandhi some years later. The first *deshbhakta* to be sent to India was the Bengali Bipin Chandra Pal, who made a lecture tour in India in 1907[172].

In late December 1904 on the first anniversary of Herbert Spencer's death[173], Shyamji announced his six 'fellowships' or travelling scholarships worth 2000 Rupees each[174]. They were to be awarded to Indians with high academic qualifications, who wished to study abroad to further their careers in independent professions in India. Shyamji specified that these generous awards:

"*...should be given on condition that the applicant agreed in writing to foreswear the high posts and big emoluments that they so persistently demanded from the Government of the country.*[175]"

In other words, an Indian graduate who had been awarded a fellowship should promise not to:

"*...accept any post, office, or service under the British Government after his return to India...*[176]"

Shyamji had 'crafted' his fellowships to be in complete contrast to the aims of the Indian Nationalist Congress, who:

"*... made it one of its chief occupations to promote its shining luminaries to big jobs carrying princely salaries.*[177]"

Shyamji's offer to students with its important condition preventing them from accepting work of any kind from the British was contrary to the traditions of the Congress. His fellowship scheme:

"*... marked the beginning of a new creed: moral condemnation of alien rule in India and non-cooperation against the foreign rule was implicit in it.*[178]"

Shyamji later offered more fellowships. The Parisian jeweller and political activist (a vice-President of the Indian Home Rule Society) Sardarsinhji Ravaji Rana (a barrister and classmate of MK Gandhi in the Alfred School in Rajkot[179]) also financed three fellowships[180] with the same conditions that Shyamji had imposed about refusing to work for the British. Rana had first met and become impressed with Shyamji in London and was converted by his ideas before he settled in Paris[181].

The recipients of these awards included[182]: Hardayal, Pal, Vinayak D Savarkar, Khudi Ram Bose, Adbdullah Suhrawardi, Sarat Chandra Mukherji, Parameshwar Lal, Madan Lal Dhingra, Sayid Abdul Majid, and Sheik Abdul Aziz. Some of these beneficiaries figure later in this text. Shyamji, Rana, and others in the Indian Home Rule Society were no longer young men. The financial aid offered by means of the travelling fellowships provided a method of bringing to London younger people who were likely to be in sympathy with Shyamji's approach to bringing freedom to India[183]. Most of them were recommended by patriots in India (e.g. BG Tilak), who did not toe the 'moderate' Indian National Congress party line.

Competition for these scholarships was keen. For example, VD Savarkar, who was to write about Hindutva in the 1920s, was one of eight successful applicants for Shyamji and Rana's awards chosen from 153 applicants[184].

Shyamji's travelling fellowships were generous. However, a notice in *Indian Sociologist*[185], suggests that the situation was not so straightforward. In addition to promising not to serve the British in any way at all after their return to India, successful candidates were to:

1. Return the sum of 2000 Rupees by a date specified at the time of agreement of the fellowship, paying interest at 4% per year.

2. Each beneficiary had to insure his life for 5000 Rupees, paying his own premium. If he were to die before repaying his fellowship, the outstanding amount of the loan would have to be paid out of the proceeds of the policy.

3. The certificate of the insurance premium mentioned above was to be given to the donor as security for the money advanced.

The fellowships were loans rather than gifts. Shyamji, a shrewd businessman, risked little financially with the terms listed above.

In addition to establishing *Indian Sociologist*, founding the India Home Rule Society, and creating the travelling scholarships, Shyamji added one more ingredient to his recipe for gaining support for India's complete independence from the British. This was the establishment of India House, which is discussed in the next chapter.

INDIA HOUSE

"... the most dangerous organisation outside India...[186]*"*

Life was not easy for Indian students in London at the beginning of the 20th century. Often, they faced racial prejudice from landlords of boarding houses and other types of accommodation[187]. Shyamji Krishnavarma decided to set up a hostel exclusively for Indian students, where they would feel welcome surrounded by other Indians, and where Indian food would always be available. The May 1905 issue of Shyamji's *Indian Sociologist* announced:

"A freehold estate has been purchased at Highgate (London), ... which according to official statistics is the healthiest suburb of London and which has the lowest death rate in the United Kingdom. The property is situated close to trams[188], within easy reach of three railway stations, and also within a few minutes walk of Waterloo[sic] Park[189], Highgate woods and Queens woods. [190]*"*

This did not become typical student accommodation. It became a focus for revolutionary ideas.

The corner plot at 65 Cromwell Avenue in Highgate contains a huge Victorian house built as part of an estate created by the Imperial Property Investment Company[191] in the late 19th century. Shyamji bought the freehold property for about £7,600[192]. It is difficult to say what this sum is equivalent to in today's money but houses like number 65 currently sell for several million pounds. This increase is not because the area has 'gone up in the world'. In Shyamji's time, it was just as desirable as it is today. An early issue of *Indian Sociologist* described:

"The house stands in its own grounds, and has at present accommodation for about twenty-five young men. Arrangements will ultimately be made to build and so take in fifty students. The Lecture Hall, Library and Reading Room are all on the same floor, thus presenting every facility for study and intercommunication. To provide recreation there is ample space for tennis courts, gymnasium, etc."

Students in receipt of travelling fellowships from Shyamji or Rana were charged one rate, and others a different one:

"The management of the establishment will be in the hands of Indians only, and the domestic arrangements will be similar to those of Ruskin College, Oxford. No alcoholic drinks will be allowed on the premises. Indian gentlemen holding Travelling Fellowships will be charged 16/- per week for board and residence, while others will be received on such terms and condition as may be specifically arranged. [193] *"*

India House was, Shyamji explained, the first attempt in the UK to create a safe, congenial residential meeting place for students from all over India. Despite the reputation for radical political agitation that the House was to gain, Pandit Bhagwandin Dube, a young student who lived there for a few weeks, wrote:

"There were a number of students who entertained a variety of opinions on political questions. Residence in the house certainly does not imply agreement with any political creed.[194]*"*

The inauguration of India House was on the 1st of July 1905, a typical English summer day with thunderstorms and almost an inch of rainfall[195]. The inclement weather did not deter many Indians and others from attending. Amongst those present were:

"… Mr. Hyndman (Social Democratic Federation), Mr. Swinny (Positivist Society), Mr. Quelch (Editor of Justice), Madame Despard (Irish Republican and Suffragette), Dadabhai Naoroji, Lajpat Rai, Madame Kame [i.e Madame Bhikaji Rustom Cama[196]: a prominent Parsi leader of the Indian independence movement], *Mr. Hans Raja, Mr. Dost Mohammad (Bar-at-Law) and many students including holders of the Indian Travelling Fellowships.*[197]*"*

The Reverend SD Bhabha (President of the Indian Christian Union) was also present[198].

Shyamji was delighted to see an old friend, the octogenarian Dadabhai Naoroji, attending, despite knowing that the Parsi gentleman was firmly wedded to the idea that India should be reformed within the British Empire. Another welcome visitor was the Irish nationalist freedom fighter Charlotte Despard. She had been to India[199] and was all in favour of the complete emancipation of the country[200]. Mr Hyndman made the inaugural speech. He began by saying that:

"...loyalty to Britain means treachery to India ... Unfortunately Indians have failed to see (the ruinous effect of the drain from India). They have hugged their chains. Even in their own associations here in London they have been too content to be patronised. The East India Association itself was captured by Anglo-Indians, ... All this it will be the high privilege of India House to largely remedy..."

Later, he pointed out that:

"From England herself there is nothing to be hoped ... It is the immoderate men, the determined men, the fanatical men who will work out the salvation of India by herself... The institution of this India House means a great step in that direction of Indian growth and Indian emancipation, and some of those who are here this afternoon may live to witness the first fruits of its triumphant success. [201]*"*

And, a few of them did witness that success he mentioned. Hyndman's words at the inauguration set the tone for what was to emerge from the people and their activities in the newly opened India House.

The opening of India House did not go unnoticed in India, where recent events (notably the Partition of Bengal) had heightened the tension between those who wanted to maintain a British led government and those who wanted Indians to rule themselves. In India:

"...The Anglo-Indian press began to denounce Shyamaji as a dangerous mischief-monger. The Congress press assumed an attitude of cold indifference, though it was often compelled to take note of the new happenings in London ... The Extremist party on the other hand ... very soon began to applaud the activities and to reproduce the writings of the budding patriot in its rapidly increasing newspapers which were then capturing the imagination of people. [202]*"*

BG Tilak and Bipin Chandra Pal[203], leading personalities in the Swadeshi and Boycott movements[204], whose ideas contrasted dramatically with those of the essentially pro-British Indian National Congress 'moderates', praised Shyamji's work in London. Like Shyamji, they believed passive resistance to be a powerful tool for ousting the British from India. Indeed, Shyamji wrote in an issue of *Indian Sociologist* that if all Indians went on strike for one week, and everyone refused to buy or sell anything that week, the British Empire would soon collapse in India[205]. Tilak wrote to Shyamji on the 14th of July 1905:

"If we have a few more workers like you in England a good deal may be done for the country, far more than we have hitherto done ... Please accept my hearty congratulations on the self-sacrificing spirit in which you have started these institutions. The free atmosphere of England gives you a scope which we never hope to get here.[206]"

The 'atmosphere' to which Tilak referred was that of freedom to act without nearly as much interference by the authorities, as was the case in heavily policed India where anyone remotely suspected of undermining British rule came under the close watch of the Indian CID and similar security organisations. Subversive activity in India was extremely risky, and often ended with imprisonment or worse. However, it was not long before India House came under the surveillance of Scotland Yard[207].

After India House opened, Tilak recommended that various students, including Vinayak ('Veer') Savarkar, Pandurang ('Senapati') Bapat, Madhavrao Jadhav, should come from India funded by the fellowships funded by Shyamji and Rana.

Bapat, a Chitpavan Brahmin, arrived in England in 1904 with a Government scholarship to study engineering. In January 1906 he read out an anti-British speech in Edinburgh. This was published later as a pamphlet entitled *India wanted Home Rule*, which caused the Government to cancel his scholarship[208]. Later, he was to become involved in bomb-making.

Before continuing the story of India House, the next chapter will introduce one of its best remembered residents, VD Savarkar.

THE MAN FROM NASIK

Vinayak Damodar ('Veer'[209]) Savarkar was born in 1883 into a Chitpavan Brahmin family at Bhagur fourteen kilometres north of the city of Nasik. The Maharashtrian Chitpavan community of Brahmins has produced many Indian freedom fighters including Tilak, the Chapekar brothers (see above) and Nanu Sahib, who was one of the leaders of the 1857 Rebellion.

Veer Savarkar (from book by Keer,D)

A much-quoted, detailed biography of Veer's life was written by Dhananjay Keer[210]. However, the lawyer and writer AG Noorani, who is critical of Savarkar and his ideas, suggested that Keer's book is hagiographical[211]. Nevertheless, Keer's informative volume and a well-packed website[212], which is sympathetic to Savarkar, provide many details of Savarkar's life.

Veer had an older brother Ganesh (aka: 'Barbarao') and two younger siblings. In 1893, severe rioting, connected with killing of cows[213] (according to the British), but this cause was disputed by leaders of 'cow-protection' organisations such as Dinshaw Petit and BG Tilak[214]. It broke out between Hindus and Muslims in the United Provinces and Bombay. The British reaction to these was expressed by the London MP Mr G Russell:

"As my hon. Friend is aware, religious riots are of almost annual recurrence in India; and the Secretary of State does not, as at present advised, think it necessary to direct the Government of India to appoint a Commission, as suggested by my hon. Friend.[215]"

Ten-year-old Veer, who was more disturbed by what was happening than Mr Russell, led a group of his fellow Hindu schoolmates on a march towards a local mosque, whose windows they broke by throwing stones. Later, Muslim boys retaliated with force, but Veer and his gang, which he had trained to be effective in conflict, were able to defeat them[216].

After attending a village primary school, Veer continued his education with Ganesh at a high school in Nasik. In 1897, when Veer heard of the Chapekar brothers' assassination of Rand in Pune and their harsh punishment, he was recovering from smallpox at his family home in Bhagur. He went to the family's deity, an effigy of Durga, and swore to complete the mission that he believed the Chapekars to have begun - to rid India of the British. A gifted writer, the young Veer also composed a ballad about the 'martyred' Chapekars[217]. So, at the tender age of fourteen, Veer began his 'crusade' against the British.

In 1899, Veer and some followers of Tilak, including Trimbak Mhaskar, Barbarao, and Raoji Krishna Page formed a society called 'Mitra Mela ('Group of Friends')'. Its aim was the complete political independence of India[218]. The group met once a week to discuss politics. Extremely well-read, Veer gave talks at the meetings about what he had been reading recently[219]. His extensive reading included works by Herbert Spencer, who had influenced Shyamji. The group also managed to convert religious ceremonies and festivals in Nasik into political nationalist functions, much to the dismay of the British authorities. Branches of Mitra Mela began opening all over Maharashtra. During a period of plague, the young members of Mitra Mela carried corpses to the cremation grounds[220]. Veer had decided that caste was unimportant in his organisation; for him all Hindus were equal. Despite organizing his society and writing much poetry (Savarkar was a born poet) and other literature, Veer did not let his school studies suffer.

Just before he matriculated, eighteen-year-old Veer married Trimbak Ramchandra's daughter Yamunabhai in 1901. Around that time, Veer passed an examination that would have allowed him to enter Government service should he ever had wanted, but his father-in-law's financial assistance allowed him to proceed to higher education instead. In 1902, Veer left to study in Pune, leaving Mitra Mela under the command of his elder brother, Ganesh[221]. He joined Ferguson College (Pune) in early 1902, aiming to major in arts[222]. His writing and oratory, which impressed but often upset many of his teachers, soon attracted a group of young men around him. Veer became a significant figure at political meetings in Pune.

In May 1904, Veer held a meeting of members of Mitra Mela from all over Maharashtra in a house in Nasik. After telling the assembled people about Italy's Giuseppe Mazzini (1805-72) and the secret organisation, Giovine Italia (Young Italy), which he had founded to undermine and remove the foreign governments (Austria and Spain) that were ruling Italy before its Unification (and birth as a sovereign state), Veer announced that the name of Mitra Mela was to be changed to Abhinav Bharat ('Young India')[223]. Its aims[224] were to spread all over India in order to extend its political and revolutionary activities, especially armed revolt.

Veer and his group, members of Abhinav Bharat, decided to boycott foreign goods. In October 1905, he suggested that the students should burn their British and other foreign clothes on the festival of Dussehra. Taking carts loaded with clothes, a procession began on the 7th of October. The clothes were covered with red powder and taken to a public space near Fergusson College[225], where Tilak joined the event. The garments were ignited whilst various men gave speeches around the bonfire. Thus, Veer became the first Indian to burn foreign cloth. His exploit led to a fine and his expulsion from his hostel at Fergusson College, but assured him both fame and infamy all over India[226].

JD Joglekar, who knew Savarkar from 1938 onwards, wrote that each branch of Abhinav Bharat was autonomous:
"The branches were only linked through the heads ... it was a federation of secret societies ... so all members were not known to one another. In fact such intimacy was avoided. The rule was rigorously

observed. The benefit derived there from ... a number of institutions, thousands of members and cache of arms were later saved...[227]"

Abhinav Bharat was run on the lines of the secret revolutionary societies as envisioned by Mazzini in Italy and others in Ireland and Russia.

In December 1905, Veer graduated, was awarded his BA degree. He had already passed the first LLB examination a year earlier. Next, he moved to Bombay where he enrolled at Wilson College to take his final law degree examination[228].

It was back in Pune that Veer came across a copy of Shyamji's *Indian Sociologist* and became aware of the travelling fellowships being offered to Indian graduates[229]. With the recommendation of Tilak, Veer applied for one of these awards. Veer received the news that he had been given one while he was in Nasik. He travelled to Pune to sign the agreement on the 20th May 1906[230]. On the eve of his departure for Europe, Veer was the guest of a large meeting in Nasik (400-500 attended[231]) to wish him farewell. He gave a speech in which he told the audience that his true purpose in travelling abroad was not to advance his personal career but to do his duty for India, the Motherland.

Savarkar left Bombay on the 26th of May on the *SS Persia*[232] of the P&O steamship company[233]. He shared a cabin with Harnam Singh, who was travelling to England to become a barrister. On board ship, Veer left his copy of a biography of Mazzini lying around in places where other young Indians were likely to find it. He had underlined passages that mentioned secret societies. In so doing, he was able to persuade other Indian students on board to join the Abhinav Bharat, the secret anti-British society that he and his elder brother had founded in 1904. When Harnam Singh became terribly seasick on board, Savarkar took care of him and told him that the aim of travelling to India should not be to become rich by practising law or joining the Indian Civil Service, but to assist in gaining the freedom of India from the British. Harnam began studying at the Agricultural College in Cirencester but soon became involved in anti-British activity.

Savarkar disembarked from the *Persia* in Marseilles, where he looked in vain for traces of his hero the freedom fighter Giuseppe Mazzini (1805-72), who lived there briefly and has been described as:

"... *the principal theorist and ideologue of patriotic movements in Europe*[234]".

Mazzini had directed an underground movement aimed at freeing Italians from their foreign rulers. From Marseilles, Veer travelled by train and ferry to London, where he was met on the 2nd or 3rd of July at the station by representatives of India House. Incidentally, Veer's travelling companion Harnam Singh also stayed at India House, but somewhat later.

Veer was admired by some of the Indians in London and disliked, and even feared, by people whose job it was to keep England and India safe from extremism. His activities in London will be revealed when happenings at India House are described below.

THE EARLY YEARS OF INDIA HOUSE

Portrait of Krishnavarma on the cover of a book by Hitesh Bhanusali

During the first three years of its existence, India House was headed by its founder and owner, Shyamji Krishnavarma. Throughout this time, he lived nearby in his own home opposite Highgate Woods but attended meetings and other activities in India House. After mid-1907, the establishment was under the supervision of SR Rana, who visited London occasionally from his home in Paris[235]. Later, it was led by Veer Savarkar. In the last days of its existence, Haider Raza succeeded Savarkar as head of the House[236]. India House was visited by many people and was home to some of these. Their names will be mentioned as the story unwinds, and I have included a list of them after the end of the main text.

According to Veer Savarkar[237], a 'disciple' of Shyamji, the Indian nationalist Lala Lajpat Rai (1865-1928), was the first paying guest at India House. Rai and the far more 'moderate' GP Gokhale (1866-1915) had been sent to London to make a last-minute appeal against the Partition of Bengal. Gokhale saw in the British connection with India

"… *an instrument ordained for India's welfare*[238]" and was, like many others of his time, a believer of Britain's benevolent intentions for India. Their appeal was unsuccessful. However, during this visit, Rai became acquainted with Shyamji and sympathetic to his ideas[239]. Later that year, Rai attended the Congress session in Benares in December 1905, at which he joined Tilak and the Bengali Bipin Chandra Pal in support of a programme to achieve self-rule by means of boycotting British goods and services.

Lajpat Rai was not overly impressed by the accommodation available at India House during his visit in August 1905:

"Arrangements at the India House were extremely unsatisfactory as Shyamji was loth to spend money on furnishing and equipping it. He did invest money in the building and bought a little furniture also, but for the rest he wanted all the expenses to be met out of the rent earned by the House. This was not easy in the very beginning. For some time an Ahmedabad barrister — one Mr. Desai — and my-self were the only lodgers at the House[240].

Dadabhai Naoroji, who had attended the opening of India House and had served as a Member of Parliament in the UK from 1892 until '95, and some other Indian candidates (including Sir Mancherjee Bhownaggree) failed to be elected in the British General Election held in January 1906. This dismayed the Indian National Congress and its followers in the UK, but pleased Shyamji, who wrote[241]:

"We are glad to observe that the Indian candidates who stood for Parliament at the present general election have not been successful. An Indian who is a student of politics and a parliamentary elector cannot but arrive at the conclusion that an Indian can never effectually promote the real interests of India by entering the British Parliament."

The first Annual General Meeting of the Indian Home Rule Society was held in India House on the 24th of February 1906[242]. The Society had 119 members by then. Once again, Shyamji took the opportunity to emphasise that the object of the Society was self-government of India by Indians, and not within the umbrella of the British Government as was advocated by 'moderate' organizations such as the Indian National Congress. Shyamji, who preferred using mass non-cooperation as a means to achieving his goal of an India governed by Indians without the

British, said he was not averse to the use of violence if it became clear that the use of force appeared to be the only effective means of gaining freedom[243].

By 1906, according to a report published in Calcutta in 1918, India House had already become notorious as a 'centre of sedition'[244]. That year, Veer Savarkar arrived in England. He had been awarded a BA degree in Bombay, and then received one of the travelling fellowships financed by SR Rana, who lived in Paris. On the 16th of March 1906, Tilak wrote to Shyamji about Savarkar:

"... among the applicants there is one Mr. Savarkar from Bombay who graduated last year, and whom I know to be a spirited young man, very enthusiastic in the Swadeshi cause— so much so that he had to incur the displeasure of the Ferguson College authorities for his outspokenness last year. He has no mind to take up Government service at any time, and his moral character is very good. [245]"

Had it not been for Tilak's recommendation of this candidate, Savarkar might not have received the scholarship.

Two months before Savarkar's arrival at India House, a public meeting was held there on the 4th of May to condemn the arrest in India of Surendranath Banerjee (1848-1925)[246]. A leading figure in the Indian National Congress[247] and twice its President[248], he was taking part in a public protest against the partition of Bengal. One of the reasons for his arrest was that he was publicly singing the patriotic anthem *Bande Mataram*, a crime in the eyes of the British authorities in India[249]. Shyamji used the occasion to once again condemn the 'moderates' such as members of the Indian National Congress. He said pointedly that although he and his Indian Home Rule Society had often been criticised by the 'moderate' party, his Society:

"...was the first to Sympathise with Mr. Surendranath Banerji, who was twice elected President of the Indian National Congress.... One would naturally expect that those who were being helped with funds provided by the Indian National Congress would be the foremost in convening a public meeting on behalf of one of their former Presidents who had been so outrageously dishonoured for advocating the cause of his countrymen ...[250]"

Soon after arriving in London, Savarkar, who was regarded as a 'firebrand' by the British authorities in India even before he set sail from India, founded his Free India Society[251]. It was modelled on his Abhinav Bharat in Pune. Unlike the latter, which was secret, The Free India Society was formed for activities that could be carried out openly[252]. It was also an institution to be used to recruit suitable people to join Abhinav Bharat[253]. His new society celebrated Indian festivals, the births and deaths of Indian patriots both historical and current, and discussed political affairs. During his years at India House, Savarkar attracted a group of young men, who fell under his influence. Its membership soon grew to over one hundred and included people such as[254]: Lala Hardayal, Senapati Bapat, Bhai Parmanand, Madanlal Dhingra, Harischandra Koregaonkar, Harnam Singh, and Virendranath Chattopadhyaya, who was brother of the poet and political activist Sarojini Naidu (a follower of MK Gandhi).

Within a week of becoming a resident at India House, Savarkar began planning a book that he wanted to write about Mazzini. Mr JC Mukherjee, then the manager of India House, was able to help him find books for his research. In this account written by Savarkar, we can capture a little of the atmosphere in the hostel in Cromwell Avenue and the helpfulness of its manager:

""*Mazzini's autobiography?" said Mr. Mukherjee. He thought deeply and replied, "I think we do have such a book in our collection." He came back with a book. I was delighted. But it was only a book of 300 pages. How can Mazzini's works be contained in such a small volume? I thought. I read the book thoroughly and noted that it was only Volume One. I showed that note to Mr. Mukherjee. He took me to the library in India House. He murmured – I try to tidy up, but the residents displace the books. He eventually found three volumes. I did not have all the six volumes, but I was very pleased with what I had. It was as if someone had found hidden treasure while excavating inside a house. I read the three volumes in a week and pressed Mr. Mukherjee for the remainder volumes. He was impressed with my sincerity and studious nature. He tried hard but was frustrated at not finding them in market. Some ten days later he came straight to my room and said, "Well Mr. Savarkar, here are the rest of the books." I thanked him from the bottom of my heart and read the remaining volumes in no time.*[255]"

Savarkar's book was completed by September 1906 and dedicated[256] to BG Tilak and the Marathi freedom fighter and journalist SM Paranjape[257]. It is a collection of translations of some of Mazzini's writings into Marathi[258]. The book on Mazzini includes a long preface by Savarkar who explained that his book was written:

"...*to show parallels between Italy and India, add some suggestive lines that the readers would be thrilled and inspired to carry out armed revolution in India also.*[259]"

To make it clear that his collection Mazzini's writings were relevant to India, he pointed out the similarities of Italy's Garibaldi and Mazzini to India's Shivaji and his mentor Ramdass, respectively[260]. In an attempt not to give the authorities in India too much of a chance to claim that his book broke the law, Savarkar avoided the use of the word "India" in his text, but highlights passages in Mazzini's writings that would clearly apply to India if the word 'Italy' was replaced by the word 'India' and 'Austria' is replaced by 'Britain'. A couple of extracts of his translations of Mazzini give a taste of what Savarkar had put in his manuscript in India House:

"*Italy is being ruled by Austria. 75,000 Austrian soldiers are controlling us. We have become a slave market. Whatever little princely states had remained have become puppets of Austrians. Italy has become a big prison guarded by Austrian soldiers. Our name has become extinct. We have no national flag. Do you think you will regain your freedom by begging? Austrians have enslaved us not for releasing us by mere petitions!*",

and:

"*God has given us the Alps on one side and the sea on the other to guard our land. Today it has been blotted with slavery. Let no one sleep in this state easily. Be determined to liberate our motherland*[261]"

And, like Italy, the Indian subcontinent has mountains (the Himalayas) "on one side" and "the sea on the other".

In December 1906, he sent the manuscript, completed with the wording "*London, India House Date 28 September 1906*" to his brother Ganesh in India, where it was published after a difficult search for a printer who was willing to risk publishing such a potentially dangerous work. It appeared on sale in India in July 1907. It was widely circulated, but soon banned.

As soon as Savarkar finished his book on Mazzini, he began work on another. This one was to be his account of the events of the Rebellion in India of 1857. He wrote:

"Once again I approached Mr. Mukherjee who had helped me with works of Mazzini. I said to him, "Can you please search for any books on the great revolt of 1857 in India? I will buy them if required. I intend to write a book on the subject." He was an elderly and experienced man. He used to attend my lectures under the auspices of Free India Society. He had even taken the oath of Abhinav Bharat.[262]"

This meant that Mukherjee had joined the London branch of Savarkar's extremely secret society[263]. He found Savarkar a copy of *Kaye's and Malleson's History of the Indian mutiny of 1857-8*. It contained little of interest to Savarkar as it was the first of six volumes. Mukherjee was able to find the rest of them in libraries around London within a week of Savarkar's request. These books, interesting as they were, only increased Savarkar's hunger for more material. Mukherjee told him that the best source of information was the library of the India Office, which controlled affairs in India. However, to enter this library, readers needed references from well-known, reliable people. This ruled out Shyamji, whose views on the Rebellion were not acceptable to the India Office, as well as to other prominent Indians in London, most of whom had not approved the 'disloyalty' of Indian soldiers during the Rebellion (and disapproved of India House).

Once again, Mr Mukherjee saved the day. Savarkar recalled that:

"He had been living in London for a number of years, was married to an English woman and had a son by her. He was Indian, but his wife was white. He was working as Manager of India House and his wife was a teacher. He had English acquaintances. He obliged, went to India Office library, found out the rules and regulations, obtained the necessary references for me and I got my reader's pass. I had warned Mr. Mukherjee not to speak about my real purpose in going to India Office library. With that precaution, I did not have much difficulty in getting my pass.[264]"

Savarkar worked diligently at the India Office library for some time. All went well until he decided to give lectures at secret meetings about the Revolt of 1857 at India House[265]. Evidently, India House harboured at least one spy, an Indian working for the British. Savarkar had been watched systematically by the British CID, who had been warned about him by similar agencies in India. Word got back to the library about Savarkar's true purpose, which was to write a book about the Revolt from the perspective of an Indian nationalist revolutionary. The security agency instructed the India Office to bar him further admission to its library[266]. After he was banned, VVS Aiyar, another resident at India House[267], helped Savarkar complete his research[268]. Aiyar, who arrived in London in October 1907[269] to study for the Bar, had taken the oath of Abhinav Bharat but was not being watched by the CID at the time. The book was eventually completed, sold in India, but was soon banned. A notice prohibiting the import of any books or pamphlets about the "Mutiny" by Savarkar was issued by the Government of India on the 23rd of July 1909[270].

In September 1906, two 'revolutionaries', Nitisen Dwarkadas, a barrister[271], and Gyanchand Varma, a law student, arrived in London from India. Both became involved with activities in India House. They opened a business called the 'Eastern Export and Import Agency' at 10 Gray's Inn Place in London. It was a 'cover' for a secret smuggling operation to infiltrate arms and anti-British propaganda into India[272]. Dwarkadas soon replaced JC Mukherjee as secretary to the Indian Home Rule Society, and then later, that role was taken by Gyanchand Varma[273], who became the secretary of the London branch of Abhinav Bharat[274]. Gyanchand came from a poor family. He was unable to pay for his sea passage to England, so he took a job as a fireman on a steamer in order to reach London[275], where he wanted to study for the Bar.

During October 1906, India House received one of its most well-known guests. On the 20th of that month, MK Gandhi arrived at Waterloo Station, having recently disembarked from a ship that had carried him from South Africa. He was met by the father of Henry Polak (Gandhi's South African associate), Lewis Ritch, and others of his followers[276]. They travelled together to India House, where Gandhi spent two nights. After that, he moved to the now long-since closed luxurious Cecil Hotel, which used to stand in the Strand. During his stay in London, he attended at least three of the Sunday evening meetings held every week at India House. These meetings were to discuss matters connected with India, to celebrate Indian festivals, and to allow Indians in London to socialise.

One of the residents of India House, Dr TSS Rajan (1880-1953), who was studying for a higher medical degree (MRCP)[277], worked at Middlesex Hospital, and lived to see India become independent, described the Sunday meetings as follows:

"In the meetings of our Association held fortnightly, at least thirty persons attended. Half of them came mainly for the Indian food that we served. During food and at all leisure hours, we used to discuss the philosophy of Indian Independence, the methods that should be adopted for gaining it, and developments in India as gleaned from Indian papers received by us ...[278]"

Some more details of the Sunday meetings at India House were given by David Garnett (1892-1981), who became a leading member of the Bloomsbury Group[279]. As a seventeen-year-old, he attended one of them during the last year of India House's existence, when it was under the spell of its then leader Savarkar:

"...we were greeted by a man standing in the garden. Dutt recognized him and was recognized, and we passed in. Later he explained, with some amusement, that the sentinel had been put there because he was a man they did not trust or want to have at the meeting inside.

Inside the building were about thirty Indians, almost all very young men, for the most part students who, like Dutt, had been sent to study law and had made about as much progress in it as he had...

... Soon after my arrival we trooped into the dining-room and Savarkar, after addressing the company in Hindi, stood up and began to read aloud. As I could not understand what he was saying, I looked about the room without paying much attention to him. The sight of those brown men, some sitting round a long table, others leaning against the walls, all listening intently to the staccato voice of the speaker, was very strange to me...

...When he had finished his chapter, the greater part of the audience went into an adjoining room and someone put a record of Indian music on the gramophone.

A woman was singing in a high falsetto voice ... The air was hot... Another Indian song followed, and another, and then Dutt was telling me that the next record was of Bande Mataram- an Indian hymn, proscribed at that time. After that, the man in the fez came up and with a teasing look at me insisted on putting on a record of The Cock of the North "as a compliment to our guest, who must want to hear some real music and can't be expected to enjoy our barbarous tunes." This was tiresome of him, but I said nothing. The man in the fez---I learned at his name was A.A[280]---then put on a record of Harry Lauder.

This was a bore, and I turned and said so to my neighbour, a tall young man with a most gloomy expression, who stood leaning against the door-post. Without replying, he walked rapidly to the gramophone, stopped it and put on an Indian record ... Presently Savarkar came in, talked to me for a while and then joined in the singing [281]"

Dutt, who introduced Garnett to India House was Sukhsagar Dutt, a younger brother of Ullaskar Dutt who had been imprisoned in the Andaman Islands, accused of his involvement in the Maniktola Garden and Muzaffarpur Bomb Case[282] (see below).

Savarkar was not friendly to Gandhi when he visited India House in 1906. He strongly disapproved of this visitor's thoughts and actions throughout his life. It is said that on one of Gandhi's visits to India House, Savarkar, who loved prawns, offered some to the vegetarian visitor, who politely refused them. Savarkar said to Gandhi:

"Well, if you cannot eat with us, how on earth are you going to work with us? ... this is just boiled fish ... we want people who are ready to eat the Britishers alive...[283]"

Incidentally, Shyamji Krishnavarma was, like Gandhi, a strict vegetarian. He preferred cooked food and had his favourite food, *mung dal* (a lentil preparation), sent from India. Also, he avoided onions and chillies[284]. Regarding food at India House, especially as it reached its final year, Asaf Ali wrote:

"Within a fortnight of our stay in India House, Rauf [Ali's brother] and I decided to move out of it. For here food served there defied description. And here were Madrasis, Mahrattas, and Punjabis, each so far apart in tastes...[285]"

Gandhi had not come to Highgate to discuss eating habits with the young revolutionary Savarkar. The future Mahatma, who had praised the work of Shyamji, wanted to confront and argue his case with Shyamji, who had been very critical of the assistance that he had offered the British during their war with the South African Boers.

On one of his visits to India House (Sunday 21st October), Gandhi spent the whole day there. During the day, he spent time talking to young Indians. In the evening, he spoke with Shyamji. One of the matters that particularly concerned Shyamji was the forthcoming election of the President of the Indian National Congress. BG Tilak, whom Shyamji admired, was one of the candidates. The 'moderate' Indian nationalists favoured Dadabhai Naoroji. Shyamji tried to persuade Gandhi to dissuade Naoroji from standing. However, Gandhi felt that Naoroji was the right man to be President. In November 1906, Shyamji wrote an article in *Indian Sociologist*, condemning Naoroji. He made comments such as:

"We have ample evidence to show that Mr. Dadabhai Naoroji is ever ready to oblige his Anglo-Indian friends at the cost of his country ... Mr. Dadabhai is allowing the great reputation he made in the past to damp down the aspirations of the Indians of today ... How long does Mr. Dadabhai Naoroji expect that the Indian people will continue to be hoodwinked by him? [286]"

Three years later, Gandhi published a booklet called *Hind Swaraj*. It was, in part, a thinly veiled criticism of the extremists like Shyamji and Savarkar[287].

SHYAMJI LEAVES INDIA HOUSE

Despite Shyamji's objections, Dadabhai Naoroji began his third term as President of the Indian National Congress at a meeting held in Calcutta in late 1906[288]. Shyamji believed, as did people in India, that although the 'moderates' had won the leadership of Congress, there was a strong swell amongst the populace towards a more revolutionary approach, to strive for complete independence from the British.

At a meeting of the Indian Home Rule Society held on the 23rd of February 1907[289], Shyamji, clearly not short of money, announced his donation of 10,000 Rupees to set up an organisation of Political Missionaries in India, and that he would be consulting so-called 'extremist' leaders such as Tilak, Bipin Chandra Pal, Ganesh S Khaparde and Lala Lajpat Rai on the organisation's *modus operandi*. Tilak thought that the new scheme should include:

"(a) Dissemination of the literature of the New School by distributing pamphlets in vernacular . . . (b) Lectures, in English and vernacular. Lectures in English in the principal towns in India by one single lecturer and provincial lectures in vernacular by provincial preachers. (c) An Annual Conference.[290]"

The "New School" was described by Shyamji's biographer Indulal Yajnik:

"The champions of this so-called new school of thought were faced with a double task ... They had to perform the negative task of attacking and destroying the poisonous weeds and the noisome growth that had been so persistently reared by the Anglo-Indian enemies and their Indian dupes. At the same time they had also to do the positive task of setting out the correct objectives and of preaching the efficient methods of self-help and all-round resistance.[291]"

The young Punjabi Lala Har Dayal, who had given up his British Government scholarship to study at Oxford, became a keen member of the new missionary movement. He had become:

"... a convinced indigenist during his sojourn at Oxford, and even before he returned to India, he was seen wearing dhoti and kurta and denouncing all things foreign ... [292]"

He submitted plans for expanding the activities of the new movement, India House, and the *Indian Sociologist*. He left for India with his sick wife in January 1908 but returned (without her) to India House later that year.

The Rebellion of 1857 began on the 10th of May. The British Government decided to celebrate the fiftieth anniversary of the outbreak of the Rebellion at a military display in London by staging a reconstruction of the 1858 attack on Delhi's Kashmir Gate, which marked the beginning of the end of the Revolt. The celebration of the British victory began with a Day of Thanksgiving on the 1st of May 1907, and festivities continued for a week.

At India House, celebrations of the outbreak of the Rebellion at Meerut began on the tenth, exactly fifty years after the uprising started[293]. On that day, Savarkar held a private celebration of the Rebellion at India House, which was attended by about fifty people[294]. On the 11th of May (1907), he organised a public meeting to commemorate the Rebellion. It was held at Tilak House at 78 Goldsmith Avenue in Acton[295], then the home of Nitisen Dwarkadas. About twenty people turned up. Gyanchand Varma was the main speaker[296]. To celebrate the occasion, Shyamji published a new edition of Richard Congreve's 1857 pamphlet on India along with his own introduction[297]. This slender volume also contains the text of Congreve's protest (dated 19th of April 1859) against a Thanksgiving ceremony performed on the 1st of May 1859. It concluded with the words:

"In the name of Humanity I publicly protest against the Thanksgiving of the 1st May, as an act at variance with our national professions as free people, repugnant to the spirit of Christianity which the nation yet recognises, and an outrage upon all the higher feelings of mankind."

The 11th of May 1907 meeting was followed soon by another at India House. The house was decorated with flowers, and decorations. The place looked like a miniature India. Portraits of Indian heroes of the Rebellion were hung above the stage in the meeting hall. A meeting was held at the house, which was attended by over 200 people. Savarkar gave a speech during which he criticised the British for calling the Rebellion of 1857 "The Mutiny", and then renamed it "The Indian War of Independence". Enamelled badges bearing the words 'Bande Mataram' were worn by students. One of these was worn by Harnam Singh, who was studying at Cirencester. He attended several meetings at India House. A Punjabi lady Dhan Devi added to the festivities by offering a handsome cash prize to Indian students who gave proof of their nationalism and valour[298].

INTRODUCTION.

IN April, 1905, I wrote in the columns of "The Indian Sociologist" that my attention had been drawn to a remarkable pamphlet under the title "India," published in 1857 by the late Dr. Richard Congreve, M.A., Honorary Fellow of Wadham College, Oxford, and founder of the Positivist Community in London. Its perusal convinced me then that Dr. Congreve was entitled to the utmost respect and gratitude of the Indian people for his noble and disinterested services rendered to India. I added at the same time that the Essay richly deserved to be reprinted and widely circulated, and that it ought to be read and re-read by every man and woman both in England and in India.

To quote the words of Mr. F. Hugh O'Donnell, formerly M.P. for Dungarvan, " Certainly some Reparation to the Dead is due before the *Jubilee of 1857* which will come in 1907," I think that this is a fitting time for reproducing the Indian pamphlet of Dr. Richard Congreve, whose love of truth was intimately connected with benevolence, and who was loved and honoured by a large number of cultured men and women of his time.

SHYAMAJI KRISHNAVARMA.

" India House,"
    65, Cromwell Avenue,
        Highgate, London, N

April 5th, 1907.

Krishnavarma's introduction to the 1907 reprint of Congreve's "India"

Over in India on the 10th of May, Lala Lajpat Rai, a lawyer and follower of Swami Dayanand, who had been present at the inauguration of India House and had stayed there[299], was arrested in India, where the British authorities were very nervous about the anniversary of the 1857 Rebellion. He was imprisoned (without being tried) in Mandalay, Burma[300]. His alleged transgression was assisting in agitation in the Punjab. He had long been under the suspicious eyes of the British authorities[301]. The British Government were 'itching' to remove Rai from the public sphere. Shyamji's biographer wrote that the British Government:

"... *knew that while the Lala keenly felt and preached aloud sentiments of national freedom and resentment against tyranny, he had as little to do as the Viceroy of India with any secret revolutionary conspiracy for overthrowing British rule in India. They cunningly made an excuse of rightful protests and growing resentment against revenue exactions to deport the Lion of the Punjab and to snuff out all inconvenient agitation in the Frontier Province ...*[302]"

The same writer added that Rai's deportation was the Government of India's:

"... *guilty conscience pricked by the memories of 1857 that intrigued* [sic] *Government into this act of insensate folly.*"

Lajpat Rai's arrest stirred up anti-British sentiments in India almost as much as the partition of Bengal had done. Shyamji, who had become friendly with Rai in London, wrote in an issue of *Indian Sociologist* published soon after the arrest:

"*To us personally the sudden disappearance of Lala Lajpat Rai from the field of operations in India under such painful circumstances has given a shock which we cannot describe in words. On almost the very day of his arrest we received a highly pathetic letter from him imploring us to do all in our power to bring the Punjabee[303] case to the notice of the British public and the foreign press. Little did he think when he penned that letter that in less than three weeks he would be arrested and deported under a cruel and oppressive regulation by the so-called civilised government of India.*[304]"

Rai's arrest was rapidly followed by a meeting of Indians in Paris on the 11th of May. Madame Bhikaji Cama, who attended the inauguration of India House, made a stirring speech condemning the arrest. This speech was published in the June issue of *Indian Sociologist*. It was then read out at a public meeting of Indians held at India House on the 7th of June[305]
.

Around this time, there was a meeting at India House during which Shyamji said that all Indians serving the British Government should be treated and regarded as enemies of India[306]. Statements such as this and Shyamji's activities at India House, especially after he had demonstrated his concerns about the arrests of Lajpat Rai and the Punjabi revolutionary Sardar Ajit Singh[307], attracted unwelcome attention from his critics in London, both in the press and in Parliament. For example, on the 30th of July 1907, a Liberal MP, Mr John Rees who had been a British Resident in two Princely States[308], said in the House of Commons:

"I beg to ask the Secretary of State for India ... whether his attention has been called to the speech made by the said Shyamaji Krishnavarma, in which he says that no concession can ever satisfy him save one, the disappearance of the alien yoke from India; and whether... the Government will consider the propriety of moving the Public Prosecutor to proceed against this person in view to his ultimate expulsion as an undesirable alien, who endeavours to debauch the loyal subjects of His Majesty.[309]"

Mr Rees wrote elsewhere that Shyamji:

"... an M.A. of Oxford, is described as the president of the Indian Home Rule Society, which is no doubt some association designed to tamper with the loyalty of young Indians in this country. Inasmuch as this person has, of course falsely, described himself, because he is a subject of a native state, as owing no allegiance to Britain, it is to be regretted that he is not deprived of the hospitality he abuses, by being expelled as an undesirable alien.[310]"

Earlier, the London *Times* wrote:

"There can be no doubt of the desire of the extremist agitators to win over the people of the feudatory [i.e. Princely] *states to their side. Indeed, this was openly avowed in a recent number of the Indian Sociologist, in which armed rebellion on their part was expressly agitated.[311]"*

Shyamji publicly objected to this wording.

One of Shyamji's reactions to the arrest of Rai and the concurrent unrest in India was to publish his translations of the French revolutionary song, *La Marseillaise* into Bengali, English, Gujarati, Hindi, Marathi, Sanskrit, and Urdu[312]. He hoped that it would be sung by all the people of India. With these translations of a song that was associated with the frequently violent activities during the French Revolution, Shyamji was not proposing the abandonment of passive resistance as a method for ousting the British from India but was also suggesting a more active approach. He did realise:

"...that even the most impassioned advocacy of Passive Resistance ... could not possibly save him from the natural consequences of publishing La Marseillaise, Madame Cama's letter about Lalaji, and other material calculated to upset the British applecart in India. He knew full well that India Office and Scotland Yard were busy closing the net around him.[313]*"*

Shyamji became increasingly aware that he was under surveillance and risked arrest. He and his wife shifted from London to Paris around about the time that his translations were published. He publicised his move in the September issue of *Indian Sociologist*, in which he explained that his sudden departure from London was precautionary:

"... it is folly for a man to allow himself to be arrested by an unsympathetic government and thus be deprived of liberty of action, when by anticipating matters he can avoid any such evils. Acting up to this principle we forestalled our enemies. It may interest our readers to know that on the earnest advice of some of our best friends, we left England practically for good, during the early part of June last, seeing that mischief was brewing, and that our political propaganda would be given a short shrift by the enemies of our country",
adding:

"Just ten years ago when our friend Mr. Bal Gangadhar Tilak and the Natu brothers were arrested we decided to leave India and settle in England, and now that another friend Lala Lajpat Rai has been deported it falls to our lot to quit England and at much expense and personal inconvenience make Paris our headquarters. We are fully convinced that no Indian who loves political freedom and ardently desires his country's emancipation from the present oppressive alien yoke is safe within the bounds of the British Empire...[314]*"*

With Shyamji's departure from London, Veer Savarkar wound up the India Home Rule Society and took over the leadership of India House[315].

BOMBS AND BULLETS

After Shyamji had shifted from London to Paris, he kept in contact with India House via SR Rana, who visited London frequently in connection with his Paris based jewellery business[316]. With Shyamji's departure from London and Veer Savarkar's installation as leader of India House, 65 Cromwell Avenue became even more of a centre of intrigue than it had been previously. Amongst other things, it became the *de facto* headquarters of Savarkar's Abhinav Bharat, an organization for which Shyamji had much sympathy and might possibly have joined[317]. Savarkar led the group, with the help of the Tamil revolutionary and law student at Lincolns Inn VVS Aiyar (vice-President) and another law student Gyanchand Varma (Secretary). Joining Abhinav Bharat was not something that the new member could take lightly, as the words of its oath of allegiance illustrate:

"In the name of God, in the name of mother Bharat and in the name of my ancestors I (Name) convinced that without obtaining the absolute political independence my country cannot obtain the glorious space amongst the Nations of the world and convinced also that political independence cannot be obtained without waging a bloody and relentless war, do solemnly declare that I shall from this moment do everything in my power even at the cost of my life to crown my country with her swaraj and solemnly swear that I shall even be faithful and true to this society. If I betray the whole or a part of this oath may I be doomed to death. Bande Mataram[318]"

The organization's manifesto was ambitious. Savarkar was actively encouraging the establishment of new branches of Abhinav Bharat all over both Europe and India. With rumours of the imminent outbreak of war (i.e. the World War that eventually began in 1914), Savarkar was keen that Abhinav Bharat should maintain strong links with Indian expatriates and, also, resistance movements in China, Egypt, Ireland, and Russia. Both Savarkar and Aiyar had made several contacts with Kemal Ataturk while he was planning to overthrow the Ottoman regime in Turkey. Savarkar 'hobnobbed' frequently with the leaders of

Ireland's Sinn Fein and hoped to organise an anti-British 'front' that would include Egypt. He even suggested blocking the Suez Canal in the event of armed rebellion in India[319].

Other aims of Savarkar and Abhinav Bharat included: teaching *swadeshi* (making, buying, and using goods made in India by Indians using Indian raw materials) and boycott (of imported goods) in India; buying and storing weapons; military training; smuggling weapons and ammunition to India; opening small factories; and persuading the members of the ranks of Indian troops to become sympathetic to the idea of overthrowing their British officers and other British people in India.

Savarkar did not share Shyamji's faith in the efficacy of passive resistance alone as a means for ousting the British. A follower of Chandragupta (founder of the Maurya Empire), Shivaji (Maratha hero), Tilak, Mazzini, and Garibaldi, he was convinced that the human mind was addicted to the idea that 'might is right'. He asked what good passive resistance would have done to stop the invasion of India by the likes of Nadir, Chengiz, Timur, and Ghazni[320]. At a meeting of the Free India Society, Savarkar maintained that passive resistance would fail in India without the backing of an army and because it:

"... *blindly assumes that the aggressor has a high sense of morality and will not resort to arms or enact new orders and ordinances.*[321]"

To illustrate what he meant, Savarkar used the then recent example of farm workers in Narbonne (France) in 1907, who used passive resistance to protest. They were suppressed by the French military[322].

Savarkar's personality bewitched the people who resided in or visited India House. His close colleague MPT Acharya[323], a resident in the house, described Savarkar as follows:

"*His personal charm was such that a mere shakehand* [sic] *could convert men as VVS Aiyar and Hardayal - not only convert but even bring out the best of them. Sincere men always became attached to him whether they agreed with or differed from him ... Not only men in ordinary walks of life but even those, aspiring to high offices, recognised the purity of purpose in him, although they were poles apart from him and deadly opponents as regards his political objectives ... Savarkar's authority was itself a discipline to others...*[324]"

Savarkar introduced several changes to life in India House. These included regular singing of *Bande Mataram*; the use of the words 'bande mataram' as a salute between members of the 'extremist' group; and every night a recitation of a vow at bed time: *Ek dev, Ek desh, Ek bhasha, Ek jaati, Ek jeev, Ek kasha* (i.e. 'One God, One nation, One language, One race, One life, One Hope')[325].

Other changes introduced to India House by Savarkar were less peaceful in intent and reflected the approach to ridding India of the British favoured by Abhinav Bharat. Some of his 'extremist' supporters joined a shooting club to improve their use of firearms. Savarkar created a 'war workshop' in the backyard of India House. There, members of his group of revolutionaries experimented with bomb-making. Often Savarkar would attend meetings of his Abhinav Bharat group with his hands stained yellow with picric acid, a chemical which explodes with mechanical contact if allowed to go dry. On one occasion Savarkar and Madan Lal Dhingra were working in the workshop when some explosive chemicals began overheating dangerously. It was Dhingra's bravery that helped Savarkar avoid a tragedy[326].

The bomb-making was guided by a bomb manual that had been obtained in Paris, translated, and then cyclostyled in London[327]. Abhinav Bharat had sent two members, Hemchandra Das and Senapati Bapat, to Paris to be taught how to make bombs by a Russian nihilist revolutionary, Nicholas Safransky[328]. Das, who had been a cattle pound inspector in India, was dismissed because of his anti-government activities in 1906. He left for England and lived in India House[329]. Bapat, also a resident in India House, had sworn a revolutionary oath in 1902 in Pune and been sent to England to study engineering. He recalled many years later (in 1960):

"I was in Paris with Hem Chandra Das of Midnapore learning bomb making. That was in 1907. From a Russian we got a manuscript in Russian on bomb making. The manuscript was in quarter sheets, about fifty in number. A Russian girl friend of mine[330]*, a student in Edinburgh University, translated it for us. I made copies of that translation. Hem Chandra returned to India with some copies. I returned to India later, in March 1908...*[331]*"*

When he reached India in 1908, he visited Das in Calcutta, where he and a few friends were busy making bombs in a room in his home. Bapat remembered:

"I helped the bomb making a little. That was on 7 April 1908."

Das, who was a superb photographer, created the illustrations for the bomb manual. Members of Abhinav Bharat in London cyclostyled more copies of it. Hotilal Varma (from Aligarh) joined Bapat and Das in London prior to smuggling the copies of the manual to India. One of these copies was presented to Tilak[332]. These manuals (and much other written matter already forbidden in India):

"... were wrapped and smuggled in the jackets of western literature classics such as Cervantes' Don Quixote and Dickens's Pickwick Papers (a cryptic wordplay on "picric papers" is possible).[333]"

Savarkar also wanted India House to become a centre for enlisting support for India's cause from outside of the UK. He wanted to publicise and project India's struggle onto the international scene. As part of this effort, he wrote articles for the *Gaelic American*, which was published in New York City. These and other articles he wrote were translated into Chinese, German, French, Italian, Russian, and Portuguese and were published in papers written in those languages[334].

The International Socialist Congress of 1907 was held in Stuttgart's Liederhalle between the 18th and 24th of August[335]. Lenin, who attended the conference, wrote:

"In Stuttgart there were 884 delegates from 25 nations of Europe, Asia (Japan and some from India), America, Australia, and Africa (one delegate from South Africa).[336]"

The delegates from India included Virendranath Chattopadhyay, SR Rana, and Madame Bhikaji Cama, all of whom were associated with India House. Their adoption as British delegates was much helped by the influence of HM Hyndman[337], who had opened the House. Savarkar, who did not attend, wanted to use the Congress as an opportunity to expose India's cause to an international forum.

Three years earlier at the Congress held in Amsterdam, Dadabhai Naoroji had proposed that there be 'home rule' in India under British supervision. Much to the disgust of most of the English delegates at

Stuttgart (in 1907), an Indian delegate Madame Bhikaji Cama[338] put forward the following motion:

"That the continuance of British rule in India is positively disastrous and extremely injurious to the best interests of India, and lovers of freedom all over the world ought to co-operate in freeing from slavery the fifth of the whole human race inhabiting that oppressed country, since, the perfect social state demands that no people should be subject to any despotic or tyrannical form of government. [339]"

Except for Mr Hyndman and the few Indian 'revolutionaries', the rest of the large British delegation opposed this motion. Clearly, the liberation of India was not favoured by most British Socialists possibly because being members of a colonialist nation gave even the most idealistic British person some sense of superiority. Later during the Congress, despite opposition from the British socialists, Madame Bhikaji Cama was able to make a speech. This was fiery and full of passion. It achieved Savarkar's aim of bringing his approach to India's struggle for independence into the international limelight[340]. During her speech on the 22nd of August 1907, she unfurled an Indian flag (bearing the words 'bande mataram'), which she and Savarkar had designed[341]. Madame Cama was aware that the Congress included Russian delegates. This was reflected in her words:

" Our people are unable to send delegations to this conference because they are so poor, but I hope one day they will be awakened, when they will follow the example of our comrades from Russia, who are fighting for freedom and to whom we send our special fraternal greetings.[342]"

What neither she nor the other Indians knew was that Vladimir Ilych Lenin, then a relatively unknown person, was sitting in the audience. However, he had taken notice of the Indian element of the Congress, as can be seen in an extract from his report written shortly after the event was over:

"... as a result of the extensive colonial policy, the European proletarian partly finds himself in a position when it is not his labour, but the labour of the practically enslaved natives in the colonies, that maintains the whole of society. The British bourgeoisie, for example, derives more profit from the many millions of the population of India and other colonies than from the British workers. In certain countries this provides the material and economic basis for infecting the

proletariat with colonial chauvinism. Of course, this may be only a temporary phenomenon, but the evil must nonetheless be clearly realised and its causes understood in order to be able to rally the proletariat of all countries for the struggle against such opportunism. This struggle is bound to be victorious, since the "privileged" nations are a diminishing faction of the capitalist nations.[343]"

It was probably this "colonial chauvinism" that caused most of the British delegates at the Stuttgart congress to support the continuation of British imperialism.

Some weeks later, Madame Cama visited the USA. During that trip, she was interviewed by many reporters. She maintained that India's hope for bringing about the end of British rule was:

"By passive resistance. We are a peaceable people and unarmed. We could not rise and battle if we would. We are preparing our people for concentrated resistance. All that is needed is unity and organisation, why, in a trice, we could have every Englishman a prisoner in his own house without a drop of blood. All that we have to do is to unify and refuse to work. In five days a bloodless overthrow could be accomplished.[344]"

By 1908, she had modified her views regarding the use of violence.

Following the Stuttgart congress, Germany's Kaiser Wilhelm II told President Wilson of the USA that the independence of India was an essential prerequisite for world peace[345]. For a long time, Germany had been looking eastwards towards the Middle East and India, which was a 'resource' that made Britain a powerful force to be reckoned with. Without Indian (and African) manpower on the Western and other fronts, the course of the First World War might have been very different. The construction of the German Berlin-Baghdad Railway, which was well underway by 1907, was regarded by the British and others as a threat to the balance of power in the Persian Gulf and beyond[346]. So, the Kaiser's words to Wilson were not simply a humanitarian wish on Germany's part, but also an expression of self-interest.

By 1908, events in India were taking a violent course. Savarkar, in London, took a great interest in these. The historian RC Majumdar wrote:

"The boycott of English goods failed to achieve the desired object of ... undoing the partition of Bengal and envisioned the political freedom of India. Hence a steadily increasing number of young men turned to revolutionary methods...There were two broad divisions among the revolutionaries... One believed in armed conflict against the British with the help of Indian soldiers ... The other believed that violent actions such as murdering officials would paralyse the Government machinery[347]"

Members of both 'divisions' created programmes for collecting arms and military training of young people. Barindra-Kumar Ghosh in Bengal (the younger brother of the famous Sri Aurobindo Ghosh) and his associates openly advocated violent revolution and guerrilla warfare. Barindra had been initiated into a revolutionary movement by Aurobindo in Baroda and sent by him to Bengal in 1902[348]. Barindra and his group set up a bomb-making 'factory' in the Muraripukur Garden house in the Calcutta district of Maniktala[349]. It was here that Senapati Bapat visited in 1908 (see above). And, it was where a copy of the bomb manual produced in India House was discovered by the police[350].

Barindra's group's first attempt at political assassination was a failure. They tried to blow up the train in which Sir Andrew Fraser, Lieutenant Governor of Bengal, was travelling on the night of 6th of December, 1907[351]. The target of another failed attempt was Monsieur L Tardivel, Mayor of the French enclave of Chandernagore. He had prevented the holding of a Swaraj meeting there a few days before the 11th of April 1908, when, whilst dining with his family, he narrowly escaped the effects of a bomb weighing two pounds. It had been placed near a window of his dining room[352].

The third bomb attempt went horribly wrong. The bomb was designed to kill Mr Kingsford, District Judge and formerly Presidency Magistrate in Calcutta. He had upset many Indians by the cold-blooded harshness of the treatment he inflicted on young perpetrators of mild offences connected with public nationalist protests. Kingsford was in Muzaffapur (Bihar) when his assassination was attempted. He had been sent there to take him away from busier areas, where there were many after his blood[353]. The *Times* in London noted that the bomb used was not imported but was much more expertly manufactured than that used at Chandernagore. Perhaps that was because the bomb-makers had been helped by the emissaries from India House, who had been learning bomb-making in Paris. However, efforts to find the manufacturer(s) of these bombs were unsuccessful. This third bomb was thrown on the 30th April towards a carriage which the bombers believed contained Mr Kingsford on his return journey home from his club. Unfortunately, the carriage that was blown-up was not that carrying Kingsford, but another vehicle, similar in appearance, carrying a Mrs Kennedy and her daughter. The latter and the coachman were killed, but Mrs Kennedy escaped with injuries[354].

The bomb that had been intended for Kingsford was thrown by Prafulla Chaki and Khudiram Bose, who had been chosen by Barindra Ghosh to execute the deed. Prafulla and Khudiaram were arrested, but the former evaded justice by shooting himself[355]. The British authorities acted quickly and indiscriminately. Explosives, bomb-making equipment, arms, ammunition, and a copy of the bomb making manual (sent from India House) were discovered at the Muraripukur Garden house. Over twenty suspected revolutionaries, including Sri Aurobindo Ghose, were arrested in and around Calcutta in May 1908[356]. Hemchandra Das, recently arrived from India House, was amongst those arrested[357]. His colleague Senapati Bapat went into hiding but was eventually arrested in 1912[358]. Incidentally, Bapat was one of three conspirators who had earlier decided to send Kingsford a bomb concealed in a book. It never blew up[359]. Tilak, who was nowhere near the scene of the crime but publicly condoned the use of bombs, was also arrested[360].

The people who had been arrested were incarcerated at, and then put on trial in Alipore (now in south Calcutta). Before the trial that began in Alipore, Sri Aurobindo and the other detainees were at first kept separated from each other in solitary confinement. They only met each other whilst waiting in court for the magistrate to arrive for a session. Later, the prisoners were allowed to live together in communal cells. Apart from Aurobindo, who was becoming absorbed in meditative matters, the other prisoners were elated at the ending of solitary confinement. In his book about the Alipore trial, Aurobindo mentioned one of the former inhabitants of India House. He noted that in:

"...the big room in which singers like Hemchandra Das, Sachindra Sen etc., were staying ... no one had a wink of sleep till two or three in the morning.[361]"

As the bomb case proceeded, violence continued in Bengal: a senior police officer was shot dead at the Calcutta High Court; a bomb blew up in Grey Street, Calcutta; and four other bombs were exploded in railway carriages[362] in and around Calcutta between June and December 1908[363].

During the Alipore trial, it became evident to the British authorities that Bapat was a close confidant of Veer Savarkar and a 'product' of India House in London. The revelation that Bapat was the procurer of the bomb manual found in Maniktala startled the authorities. They immediately assumed that the bomb plot that had been designed to kill Kingsland was planned and controlled by India House. Consequently, police surveillance of 65 Cromwell Avenue intensified[364].

Sometime in 1908, while there was fighting between Spanish and local Moroccan forces in Morocco, Savarkar sent two of his followers, Sukhasagar Dutt and another young Bengali, to Morocco to learn military tactics by fighting alongside the Moroccan forces led by Abdul Krim[365]. The mission was a failure; the two men were unable to join Krim's forces. Young David Garnett, whose description of India House is quoted above, lent Dutt his Winchester rifle to use when he reached Morocco. This weapon was confiscated by the customs in Gibraltar, and eventually returned to Garnett, who recalled:

"*Some months later I succeeded in getting my rifle returned from Gibraltar ... When it turned up I was surprised to discover that a Browning pistol had been sent back with it. Dutt begged me to keep it. I noticed, however, that the serial number, by which it could be identified, had been filed off. I asked him why and was told that the pistol was one of a batch, some of which had been smuggled to India, and that its connection with the others might be traced. When, however, I took the pistol to pieces to clean it, I found the serial number on the barrel had not been removed...[366]*"

Meanwhile back in London on Sunday the 10th of May 1908, a few days following the Muzaffarpur bombing, India House celebrated 'Red

Blood Day of the Meerut Uprising'[367]. Invitations to the meeting that was held at India House at 4 pm were printed in red ink[368] and sent to Indians all over England. As at the celebration the year before, India House was decorated with flowers and lights. Inside, the lecture hall was also decorated with flowers and incense was burnt[369]. The job of organising the meeting and decorating India House was allotted to Madan Lal Dhingra and Harnam Singh, who had travelled to England with Savarkar. The meeting opened with Gyanchand Varma singing *Bande Mataram.* Then, VVS Aiyar recited a national prayer. The song and the recitation excited the audience, who were then treated to a stirring speech by Savarkar.

The purpose of the meeting, orchestrated by Savarkar, was to celebrate many of the important leaders of the 1857 Rebellion such as Nana Saheb, and others including Emperor Bahadur Shah, the last Mughal emperor, who was accused by the British of aiding and abetting the Rebellion[370]. The meeting lasted four hours. About 100 people attended. They came from all over the UK, from as far away as Scotland. Madame Bhikaiji Cama was present and took the opportunity to raise the flag that she and Savarkar had designed. Savarkar read a four-page pamphlet entitled *O' Martyrs!* Its tone may be judged from these brief extracts:

"*... For the war of 1857 shall not cease till the revolution arrives, striking slavery into dust, elevating liberty to the throne...*

... The war began on the 10th of May 1857 and is not over on the 10th of May 1908, nor can it ever cease till a 10th of May to come, sees the destiny accomplished, sees the beautiful Ind[sic] *crowned either with the lustre of Victory or with the hallow of martyrdom...*

... With limited means you sustained a war, not against tyranny alone, but against tyranny and treachery together.[371]"

Other Indian speakers gave talks on the exploits of various Indians who had fought heroically in the past. For example, Rafiq Muhammad Khan, studying for the Bar at Lincolns Inn[372], spoke about Raja Kunwar Singh, and Hemchandra Das, who was on the point of leaving for India (see above), spoke about Rani Laxmi Bai of Jansi. Mr Master[373], a Parsi member of Abhinav Bharat also spoke[374].

After the speeches, many of those present took pledges to forego various pleasures and to contribute money to a "Fund for the Heroes and Martyrs of 1857". Madame Cama and Mr Rana, both over from Paris, donated large sums of money. Many Indian professionals (doctors, lawyers, journalists, etc.) and businesspeople along with their families vowed to observe a month of sacrifice for the cause of the freedom of India. Enamel badges commemorating the 1857 rebellion were issued and proudly worn by students and others. Harnam Singh wore his badge at the Agricultural College in Cirencester, where he was studying. He was expelled because he, like other Indian students in England, refused to stop wearing the badge[375]. Near the end of the proceedings, chapatis were offered to the people attending and tikkas (marks of coloured paste) were applied to their foreheads[376]. The significance of the Indian bread is that chapatis were sent from village to village during the Rebellion, possibly as signals to encourage its spread. These chapatis, which moved across India faster than the British mail, but contained no messages, disturbed the British, who were mystified by them[377].

Savarkar's pamphlet, which received wide attention internationally, was only one of the publications he produced in 1908. Ever since he had completed his book on Mazzini, Savarkar had been researching material (in the India Office Library until he was no longer admitted) for, and writing (in India House) a book about the Rebellion of 1857. As described already, he did much of his research at the India House Library until the reason for his interest in the events of 1857 and '58 was discovered by the British authorities. His *History of the Indian War of Independence 1857* was originally completed in 1908, written in Savarkar's mother tongue, Marathi. The history was written with a specific purpose. Writing in *Talwar*, an Abhinav Bharat paper published in Paris, Savarkar explained:

"... *that his object in writing this history was, subject to historical accuracy, to inspire his people with a burning desire to rise again and wage a second and a successful war to liberate their motherland. He also expected that the history should serve to place before the revolutionists an outline of a programme of organisation and action to enable them to prepare the nation for a future war of liberation. It would never have been possible to preach such a revolutionary gospel publicly throughout India or carry conviction so effectively as an illuminating illustration of what had actually happened in the nearest past would do.*[378]"

As such, it presented difficulties to those who wanted to publish it[379]. Unsurprisingly, the Abhinav Bharat tried without success to have an English version of what was essentially an anti-British text published in England or even in France. The Marathi manuscript was sent secretly to India, where it was also impossible to find a printer. Eventually, it was published and printed badly in Germany, where the type setters were unfamiliar with Indian scripts. Later, several editions of the book were published in various places including Holland. Copies were smuggled into India by disguising them with misleading covers or placing them in secret compartments of suitcases. Many years after it was written, copies of its 5th edition were distributed to members of Subhash Chandra Bose's Indian National Army who were fighting alongside the Japanese in the Second World War[380].

A police report noted that sometime in June 1908, a "Hindu" (i.e. an Indian) studying at London University gave a lecture at India House about making bombs. The speaker was a Dr Desai[381]. He described their ingredients and how to use them[382]. In the middle of the same month, Tilak was arrested in Bombay in connection with his writings relating to the bomb blast at Muzaffarpur. After a trial lasting over a week, he was sentenced to deportation (in Mandalay, Burma) for six years[383]. This outraged Indians all over the world. That autumn, many Indians congregated in London to appeal to the Privy Council against the deportation of Tilak.

About one month after the celebrations, Savarkar visited Paris, where he met Shyamji Krishnavarma briefly[384]. He also persuaded many Indian businessmen in that city to take solemn vows of allegiance to his secret revolutionary organisation[385]. Soon after this, in July 1908, there was a meeting of the inner council of the London Branch of Abhinav Bharat[386]. It was held at the home of its Secretary, Barrister Gyanchand Varma, in Warwick Street in London's Soho district. Varma, holding a revolver in his hand, took the solemn vow of Abhinav Bharat. According to JD Joglekar, the vow was repeated by Madan Lal Dhingra, HS Koregaonkar, Savarkar, Baba Joshi, Sen, Harnam Singh, Khan, Kashi Prasad Jayaswal, and a few others. After these people made their promises, they elected Savarkar as the Head of the branch. Jayaswal had been sent to study law in England, where he arrived in 1906. A close associate of Savarkar and VVS Aiyar, he left England in

1910 and on his way back to India he stopped for a while in Egypt, where he made strongly anti-British statements. By late 1910, he had become an advocate in the High Court of Calcutta[387].

A 'moderate' leader of the Indian National Congress GK Gokhale (1866-1915) happened to be in London at around this this time[388]. He was in London in connection with the Morley-Minto reform proposals for India (which resulted in the Indian Councils Act of 1909), which were designed to capture the hearts of 'moderate' members of Congress. In connection with these reforms, which offered some representation in the Government of India to compliant Indians, Motilal Nehru (father of Jawaharlal) said:
"They are ... just the opposite of reforms.[389]*"*
Like both Savarkar and Tilak, Gokhale was a Chitpavan Brahmin. However, his approach to reforming India differed considerably from that of the other two men. Gokhale, who was the most important Indian leader in London at the time, refused to preside over a meeting held to protest against Tilak's deportation. Some hot-headed members of the revolutionaries in London considered ending the 'cowardly' Gokhale's life, but Savarkar counselled them against this idea[390]. The meeting was held in Caxton Hall and presided by Mr Parekh. A resolution was passed condemning Gokhale's attitude to the protest against Tilak's treatment. In all fairness to Gokhale, it should be recorded that when he heard of Tilak's sentence, he immediately appealed to the Secretary of State for India Lord Morley, expressing his discomfort at Tilak's treatment and promising to do all he could to secure his release or, at least, mitigation of his sentence[391].

At about this time, there were two new arrivals at India House: Changeri Ramarao and Harischandra K Koregaonkar. Both attended meetings at India House. Koregaonkar, a Marathi, became a friend of Savarkar, joined the Free India Society, and contributed much to the activities in the House[392]. Later, both men were to provide evidence to the police when Savarkar was arrested.

Ramarao, who came to England to study Sanitary Science, mixed with the Indian revolutionaries. When he returned to India in early 1910, his baggage was examined in Bombay. It was discovered that he was carrying an automatic pistol with eighty rounds of ammunition.

These were concealed in the false bottom of one of his cases along with several copies of Savarkar's book on the 1857 rebellion as well as instructions for making bombs[393]. Under police questioning, he revealed information damaging to Savarkar and his group. He was put in prison for two years.

HK Koregaonkar became a student at the Central Technical College in Kensington (now incorporated into Imperial College[394]) possibly as early as 1906. When he returned to Bombay in August 1909, he revealed much information, possibly under duress, about India House and its activities to the police in that city. After that, he travelled to Gwalior, a free man[395].

The last three months of 1908 were busy for Savarkar's Free India Society. Various important nationalist leaders arrived in London. They included: Lala Lajpat Rai, G Narang, Bipin Chandra Pal, GB Khaparde, and RV Karandikar[396]. The latter two were in London in connection with the Tilak appeal. Lajpat Rai, who arrived on the 16th of September, was put up at India House[397].

On October the 16th, an Anti-Partition (i.e. of Bengal) Day or "Indian Nation Day" was held, at which some of these men spoke. This took place in Caxton Hall, where a meeting about the Indians in South Africa occurred later the same day. Savarkar was amongst those who gave speeches that day. The proceedings began with the large group singing *Bande Mataram*. Then, Lajpat Rai, who was the chairman, made a long speech, in which he said he wanted to see India free from British domination[398]. That same day, there were also Partition Day commemorations, during which many shops in India were closed. Five days later, the trial of Sri Aurobindo commenced at Alipore[399].

In November 1908, Savarkar gave a lecture on the subject *Are We really Disarmed?* He pointed out that there were enough arms and ammunition in India that could be used to seriously endanger British power in India, should it be possible to enlist the aid of the Indian Army and the armies of the Princely States[400]. Speeches like this could hardly have endeared India House and its associates to the British authorities, who were already keeping a close watch on them.

On Sunday the 20th of December, a conference of Indians was held at Caxton Hall[401]. Apart from Indians, there were also some Egyptian nationalists attending. Amongst the Indians present were[402]: Dadasahib Khaparde, Madame Cama, Gyanchand Varma, VV Aiyar, Sir Aga Khan, Dr Kumarswami, Savarkar, and many others. The Indian national flag designed by Madame Cama and Savarkar hung above the speakers' platform and the proceedings began with singing *Bande Mataram*. The meeting passed several resolutions. According to the report published in the *Times* of London, these included:

"... *loyal acceptance of the ideal of Swaraj, or absolute and complete independence, as the ultimate goal of the people of India...*",
and:

"... *the boycott movement ... is necessary and essential to the regeneration of India...*",
and regarding the Morley reforms[403], which were almost fully formulated, they:

"... *are conceived on the wrong lines, and calculated to accentuate differences and to encourage self-seeking on the part of individuals and political parties both in England and India.*[404]"
About Swaraj, Savarkar emphasised that its true meaning was absolute political independence. Just before the Swaraj resolution was passed unanimously, he reminded the meeting of injustices in India:

"*Before passing this resolution just bring before your mind's eye the dreadful prison walls, and the dreary dingy cells.*[405]"

Just over a week later, on the 29th of December, there was another meeting at Caxton Hall[406]. This time it was to celebrate the birth anniversary of Guru Govind Singh (c.1660-1708), founder of the Khalsa, the Sikh warrior community. The meeting began with a rendition of *Bande Mataram* and other patriotic songs including *Priyukar Hindustan*, written by Savarkar. A banner with the words "Honour to the memory of Shri Guru Govind Singh – prophet, poet, warrior" hung behind the chairman's place. The meeting, which was chaired by Bipin Chandra Pal, attracted many Indians: Hindus, Muslims, and Sikhs. Professor Gokul Chind[407] gave a long speech describing Govind Singh as being not only an active resister of oppression and injustice, but also the creator of a nation. Other speakers included Lala Lajpat Rai, Bipin Chandra Pal, and Gokul Narang[408]. After these men had spoken, Savarkar took the stage and made a stirring speech. Asaf Ali, who was connected with India House, later wrote (while in India):

"Nor is it an exaggeration to say Savarkar is one of the few really effective speakers I have known either here or in England ...[409]*"*

Public meetings like these attracted the attention of the British press, which was not favourable to sentiments expressed at them. The *Standard* newspaper commented:

"... it is beyond question that not a few of the highly intelligent Indian students in our universities and reading for the Bar, are striving their utmost by such means, particularly to accustom the minds of the young generation to the idea of armed revolt.[410]*"*

Reports such as these put India House into the public limelight and attracted even more unwanted attention from the British police.

The flag designed by Madame Cama and Veer Savarkar
(photo taken in Bhavnagar)

Before ending this account of the year 1908, mention must be made of a Russian revolutionary visitor to India House. He was brought to meet Savarkar by the British Anarchist and Communist Guy Aldred[411], who ran the Bakunin Publishing House and published Shyamji's *Indian Sociologist* for a while. The Russian had three or four meetings with Savarkar lasting from half an hour to three hours. Madan Lal Dhingra and Aldred attended them. It was only in 1937, after he had been released from prison in Ratnagiri, that Savarkar revealed the identity of his Russian visitor: Vladimir Ilych Lenin[412]. H Srivastava, who is the only writer that I have come across who mentions these meetings, dates them March 1909. However, it seems that Lenin was only in London for a brief period in May 1908[413], and then not again until 1911. It is possible that Savarkar had mis-remembered the date so many years later.

A MAN FROM THE PUNJAB

"The main master planner of the revolutionary movement in England was Shyamji Krishna Varma and his pilot was Vinayak Damodar Savarkar and Madan Lal Dhingra was its flag bearer. India House became the platform and the launching pad, wherefrom the plane of revolutionary nationalism took off.[414]
"

Despite being its 'flag bearer', Madan Lal Dhingra ('Madan Lal'), who was born in Amritsar in the Punjab in about 1883, did more to bring about the downfall of India House than any of its other visitors or residents. This chapter describes his life until 1908, by which time he had been in London for two years.

Madan Lal was the seventh-born of the eight children, and one of the seven sons, of Dr Ditta Mal, an eye surgeon who qualified in Lahore. The doctor was highly respected and very wealthy, owning six carriages. He was the first Indian to own a motor car in Amritsar[415]. Madan Lal's family were very loyal to the British. Madan Lal's father was on very good terms with important British officials such as Dunlop Smith, a senior administrator in the Punjab, and WH Curzon Wyllie, who had had dealings with Shyamji Krishnavarma during his time as a Diwan. Wyllie became aide-de-camp to the Secretary of State for India after 1901, when he returned to London from India[416]. Some say that it was Wyllie who persuaded Lord Morley to adopt unrestrained, harsh measures in India[417]. As an example of the family's loyalty to the British it is enough to note that in 1909 one of Dr Sahib Ditta Mal's sons, Dr Behari Lal Dhingra showed Dunlop Smith a:
"...sketch of a scheme he had for the establishment of a good residential school for the sons of well-to-do Indians ... where the students would be made 'God-fearing and loyal to the Crown'...[418]*"*

Three of Madan Lal's older brothers studied in London, where they qualified as barristers or medical professionals. One of the other brothers became a merchant in Amritsar and another, a barrister, a *Munsif* (lawyer) in Jammu. His youngest brother, who was in London at the same time as Madan Lal, also became a barrister before returning to practise in Amritsar and then Lahore. His only sister married a wealthy landlord but did not take on a profession. All of Madan Lal's siblings were, like their parents, extremely loyal to the British. For example, after the Muzzaffarpur bomb incident, Chaman Lal, the fourth son of Dr Ditta Mal, who was a barrister and Official Receiver for the High Court of the Punjab, published a letter in the press condemning the outrage and the secret activities of revolutionaries. In addition, he praised the rule of the British and hoped it would continue in India.

Madan Lal began his education at Mission High School in Amritsar. He passed his Intermediate Examination at Municipal College in that city, and then moved to Government College in Lahore, where he began studying science. In Lahore, he became interested in politics. During the period, 1900 to '06 when Madan Lal was a student in the Punjab, there was much political turmoil, especially in the lead up to and the wake of Lord Curzon's Partition of Bengal (1905). The Punjab Land Alienation Act of 1900[419] caused much distress and confusion in a part of India where agriculture has always been important. Both the Swadeshi and Boycott movements had affected the Punjab. Mass meetings and public burning of foreign goods were becoming common. As a student in Lahore, Madan Lal was studying amid revolutionaries. He was:

"… influenced by the political struggle for Indian Independence led by Bal, Lai, Pal. At this time revolutionary activities in the institutions of Lahore and Amritsar were on the peak. Lai, Lala Duni Chand, Dr. Satpal, Dr. Saifuddin Kitchlew, Lala Hardayal, Sham Lai, Sohan Singh Pathak (Patti), Sukhdev, Teja Singh, etc. were studying in Lahore.[420]"

Madan Lal became involved in revolutionary activity in Lahore. This led to his expulsion from Government College much to his father's dismay. His father brought Madan Lal back to Amritsar, hoping that this would deaden his interest in politics. Very soon after returning to his family home, Madan Lal decided to reject his family's help and set out to make his own living.

First, he joined the Kashmir Settlement Department as a clerk. He left after six months after having been treated so badly by British members of staff that he took a strong dislike to 'Britishers'. Next, he joined the company of Rai Bahadur Daulat Ram, a distant relative, at

Simla-Kalka Road as a tonga driver. This job was short-lived and followed by work as a labourer in a factory, where he tried to organize a trade union. This led to his dismissal. He returned home for a brief spell to see his mother, who was suffering ill-health. It was not long before he set off again. This time, he became a 'lascar' (a worker on a ship)[421]. During his time at sea, he visited Burma and Sri Lanka, but soon got fed up with this roving life[422]. He returned to India to his older brother Dr Behari Lal Dhingra, who was Chief Medical Officer[423] in Sangrur (Jhind State, now part of Haryana).

Dr Behari suggested to Madan Lal that he should continue his studies either in India or in England, where he had received his medical training. England was preferred because a degree obtained there led to better jobs in India than could be obtained with an Indian one. Behari persuaded his father to arrange for Madan Lal to study in England.

In June 1906, Madan Lal boarded a ship in Bombay, the *SS Macedonia*[424] bound for London. He travelled on the same ship[425] as HK Koregaonkar, who would eventually be involved with Madan Lal in a momentous event. Madan Lal arrived in London at about the same time as Veer Savarkar. On the 19th of October, he joined University College (London) as a student of engineering. Unlike previous activities in his life that ended prematurely, Madan Lal managed to complete his Diploma of Engineering in 1909.

Soon after his arrival in London, Madan Lal became involved with activities centred around India House. A college friend had introduced him to the house in Highgate. He visited it regularly to attend meetings but took little part in the discussions held there. Exposure to racism made him sympathetic to what was going on in India House. He had experienced racial prejudice: whilst working in the Kashmir Settlement Department; when the Australian authorities refused to allow him to emigrate there; in articles in the British press; and as a lascar.[426].

Sometime after his arrival in London, Madan Lal's brother Kundan Lal Dhingra visited London on one of his frequent business trips to the city. The two brothers met. After Kundan Lal had enquired how his brother's studies were going and had been assured that all examinations had been passed, Kundan Lal said that his father was unhappy with

Madan Lal's political activities in London. He emphasised that their family had good relations with the British and their father did not want Madan Lal to jeopardise them. Madan Lal made it clear that he would not cease his political work in London, even if, as Kundan Lal had threatened, the family were to cut off all ties with him. It was at this time that Madan Lal revealed that he proposed to live in India House. He did so from April to October 1908 and for a short time in early 1909[427]

In December 1908, Madan Lal, fed up with the racism of the British, decided that he was prepared to sacrifice his life for India. He wanted to kill as many English people as possible. His friend Koregaonkar had shared the idea with him of blowing up one of the steamships of the P & O Line that plied between England and India. Madan Lal's plan to kill Lord Curzon failed when he spotted two photographers close to his target[428]. Halfway through 1909, Madan Lal carried out an act that seriously affected the fate of India House and the people associated with it.

A FATEFUL YEAR

By the beginning of 1909, some of the men at India House became interested in arranging military training including shooting skills. A few of them had tried joining shooting clubs in London but were not admitted because of the colour of their skin. Because of this, some of them went to a gambling house where prizes were given for hitting targets with shots from guns. On the 14th of January 1909, a miniature rifle range was installed at India House. Dr Rajan joined a London polytechnic college, which offered a wide range of subjects including shooting and photography. He became skilled at shooting, both with cameras and with revolvers[429].

Govind Amin, who had lived in South Africa from 1901 for four or five years, arrived as a boarder in India House in August 1908. He was by then studying engineering at a polytechnic in London. Govind, who managed to acquire a batch of Browning pistols with the help of a group of anarchists with whom he met, took followers of Savarkar's Abhinav Bharat to Fairyland, a public shooting range in central London, to improve their skills[430]. This place was owned by Henry Stanton Morley, who described it as:
"...an exhibition of automatic machines and a shooting range at 92, Tottenham Court Road.[431]"

India House also became involved with smuggling arms to India. Browning pistols were obtained in France and then packed in the hidden compartments of suitcases with false bottoms. Some arms were sent with Mirza Abbas and Sikandar Hayat Khan[432]. Others were sent with Chatturbhuj Javerbhai Amin, brother of Govind Amin. Both had arrived in England in 1907. Chatturbhuj, a student of weaving, had been a cook at India House. As he was good at dodging detectives, a police report (dated 1911) was uncertain as to whether he had really smuggled any arms into India[433]. Another account relates that he was successful[434].

On the 12th of January 1909, an Indian man assaulted Sir William Lee Warner in a London street[435]. In 1907, Lee Warner, who had been a senior civil servant in India, was chosen to head a committee to investigate the situation of Indian students in British universities because of concerns about their involvement in revolutionary activities, especially at India House. The committee, which included WH Curzon Wyllie and other die-hard imperialists amongst its members, operated in secret, but had to interview Indian students. This led to unwanted 'leakage' of their clandestine activities. In October 1907, the *Indian Sociologist* published the committee's intentions, pointing out how intrusive it was:

"*... what a careful analysis of our daily life is here given ... Let every Indian realise that the eye of the India Office is on him every moment, and the prestige of the "Government" will surely be enhanced...*"

The committee suggested that a government-run student hostel should be set up to compete with, and possibly replace, the troublesome one in Highgate[436]. Lee Warner was therefore not popular amongst those who were sympathetic to India House and its ideas.

On the 26th of January 1909, a man calling himself 'R Sarma' turned up at the India Office to request an interview with Lee Warner. He left after being told that Lee Warner was too busy to receive him. On the 1st of February, while he was walking from the India Office to the Athenaeum Club, Lee Warner was approached by 'Mr Sarma', who asked him to receive the letter, which he had been unable to deliver when he had visited the India Office on the 26th of January. Lee Warner refused it and told him to deliver it to the India Office. Annoyed, the Indian struck Lee Warner on his leg with a walking stick, without inflicting much damage. The victim asked some onlookers to act as witnesses. His attacker refused at first to give his real name and address. He was Basundev Bhattacharya of India House, Cromwell Avenue, Highgate, and was brought to trial at Bow Street.

Basundev was believed to be the person, 'Mr Sarma', who had tried to see Lee Warner on the 26th of January and struck him the 1st of February. During the trial, Lee Warner denied that he had said to his attacker things like "*Get away you dirty nigger*". The defendant alleged that on the 19th or 20th of January, Lee Warner had called Basundev's friend Kunjalal Bhattacharya "*the son of a pig*" when he had presented a petition to the India Office official. Kunjalal then told the court that on one occasion he had tried to give Lee Warner a letter as he was entering his club. Lee Warner then said to him:

"Don't be rude to me; this is not India."

The magistrate believed that because Basundev was in an excited state following the insult his friend had received, he had struck Lee Warner. Consequently, Basundev was let off lightly without a prison sentence[437]. Whether or not the British official made hurtful insults as described is irrelevant because, sadly, it was not unusual for Indians to be at the receiving end of racist comments[438].

A few days after the trial was reported, a long letter was published in the London *Times*[439]. It was written by someone who signed himself or herself as 'Corruptio optimi pessima', which loosely translated means 'the corruption of what is best is the worst tragedy'. The writer complained about the relative impunity of Indian revolutionaries in London as compared with those in India. The letter continued with the description of a plan, published in the *Indian Sociologist* of December 1908, which proposed erecting monuments at India House. These monuments were to commemorate the two men who blew up the people at Muzaffarpur and the two men who killed an informer, Gossain, in Alipore Jail in August 1908. The writer also mentioned that scholarships in the names of these four Indian 'martyrs' were under consideration. The letter pointed out that the assailant of Lee Warner gave his address as India House, and while the nature of the offence was not grave, it was inexcusable that India House was proposing to celebrate the lives of four men, who had committed murders. The letter writer concluded by saying it was high time that the authorities acted against India House and its members.

From his home in the Passy district of Paris, Shyamji Krishnavarma wrote a reply to the letter by 'Corruptio optimi pessima'. It was published in the *Times* on the 20th February 1909. After pointing out that British oppression in India had forced people to commit violent acts, he wrote about India House, which he informed the reader was his own freehold property:

"… I may be permitted to say, as a barrister of 25 years' standing, that according to English law I can erect a monument in honour of anyone or do just what I like within its walls on the principle that an Englishman's house is his castle, so long as no nuisance or illegal act is

committed on the premises, there being no distinction between an Englishman or a foreigner in this respect."

He concluded his letter, expressing his friendship for the many Englishmen he had met while he lived for many years in England, but warning all English people not to risk their:

"...kith and kin by allowing them to go to India in these troubled times, since every Englishman who goes there for exploiting that country directly or indirectly is regarded as a potential enemy by the Indian Nationalist Party and its supporters...[440]"

At around this time, a letter written by Virendranath Chattopadhyaya, a barrister who frequented India House, was published in the *Times*. He wanted to distance himself from Shyamji's approach to gaining independence. He wrote:

"... Mr Krishnavarma ... has begun to preach secret political assassination as one of the justifiable methods of the Nationalist. He has condescended to abuse Englishmen in the same coarse manner as some of them abuse us. I do not believe in assassination, nor do I admire abusive language...[441]"

He followed this by saying that if he were ever to advocate the violent methods he objected to, he would return to India and not seek refuge, as Shyamji had done, in a "safe retreat" in a European city. On the 20th of February, Shyamji replied to these pointed remarks with their implications of cowardice on his part as follows:

"... a division of labour is absolutely necessary in almost all departments of human activity ... we have taken upon ourselves the task of preaching, while that of practising is left to others ...",
adding:

"...We have no pretensions to the glorious work done by men like Mazzini for the emancipation of their country, but it is our earnest desire to follow their example and to act up to their teachings as far as possible ...[442]"

Unlike Mazzini, Shyamji moved from one country to another to avoid arrest. (About a year later, Chattopadhyaya wrote a letter apologising to Shyamji for his criticisms[443].)

Shyamji's letter of the 20th of February, published in the *Times*, evoked a response from Virendranath Chattopadhyaya, then living at 78

Lancaster Road, which was published in the *Times*[444]. While respecting Shyamjis's intellect and integrity, the writer suggested that Shyamji should not be called a 'Nationalist. He felt that name should be reserved for leaders such as Tilak, Bipin Chandra Pal, Sri Aurobindo, and Lala Lajpat Rai. These men, the writer pointed out, desired a peaceful evolution of India without resort to murder and assassination. They advocated passive resistance without breaching India's criminal code. Chattopadhyaya concluded his letter by saying that if a few young men had been driven to mindless violence, it was not the fault of the Nationalists, nor Krishnavarma, but of the British Indian administration, which had violated the normal rights of British citizens (i.e. Indians living in India).

On the 28th of February 1909, Veer Savarkar's brother, Ganesh, was arrested in Pune. He was charged with aiding and abetting treason against the King, for which death was a possible punishment[445]. The main charge against Ganesh was his provocative poetry![446] Some days later, his home was thoroughly searched. Ganesh's biographer describes what was discovered:

"... *they found a secret passage in the wall. A heap of papers was hidden there. Amongst the papers written in purple ink was an illustrated bomb manual, a 68 page book with various addresses several letters and eleven copies of a pamphlet entitled "Two historically significant essays". The bomb manual had been sent from London by Tatyarao* [i.e. Veer Savarkar] *and was exactly similar to the bomb manual found in the Maniktola case in Calcutta. In his judgement, Justice BC Kennedy was to describe this manual thus, "It is a very complete and detailed document giving minute instructions for the making of a very large number of explosive bombs and fuses." The address book contained addresses of Abhinav Bharat members as also the address of Hemchandra Das who was an accused in the Maniktola conspiracy case. The confiscated letters were written by Tatyarao, VM Bhat, Lakshman Vasudeo Brahme (Satara) and Anandanand (Bengal) among others. The pamphlet had its origins with Tatyarao in London. It contained the manifesto released by the Begum of Bhopal during the 1857 uprising and referred to the British King as a tyrant and murderer ... The raid marked the beginning of the end of the Abhinav Bharat.*[447]"

Ganesh's case and his brother Veer's connections with it intensified the police's attention on India House and Veer's activities in London.

In the early summer of 1909, a thirty-year-old Maharashtrian called Kirtikar, who spoke several Indian languages because he had been a translator in the High Court of Bombay, came without introductions to India House[448]. He talked Veer into permitting him to live at the House. Very soon after his arrival, he enrolled as a student of dentistry in a London hospital. It was not long before some of the other residents noticed that the new dental student had begun returning home late at night, lazing in bed, and having breakfast late.

Kirtikar struck up a friendship with an English maid who worked at India House. Food preparation began to suffer as a result because Kirtikar had set up the maid in nearby accommodation, which he paid for. Dr Rajan, who lived in the House and attended the same hospital as that in which Kirtikar had enrolled, discovered that the dental student was no longer attending classes at the dental school. Rajan informed VVS Aiyar, and it was soon realised that unlike all the other members of India House, Kirtikar was not being followed by agents from Scotland Yard.

One day when Kirtikar was taking his girlfriend, the maid, to the theatre, Aiyar opened his room (using a master key) and searched it. He discovered a report about activities in the House, which Kirtikar had prepared for the police. He took this to Rajan and Savarkar, who then realised that Kirtikar was a police spy. After considering what to do with Kirtikar, including the possibility of expelling or killing him, it was decided to make use of him. Later that day, Aiyar confronted Kirtikar with a revolver and made him understand that his spying activities had been uncovered. After begging for his life, the false dental student agreed to continue preparing police reports, but on condition that they could only be sent on to Scotland Yard after they had been edited and vetted by Aiyar. He agreed, and Scotland Yard began receiving reports that were designed to hoodwink them[449]. Kirtikar remained at India House for many more months and stuck to his agreement.

Soon after Kirtikar's unmasking as a spy, MP Tirumalachari, a Tamil from Madras, arrived at India House saying that he was impoverished and had travelled from India as a third-class passenger[450]. He said that he had worked for *India*, a weekly published in Pondicherry and Madras, and had learned of India House through its pages. Penniless, he said he was prepared to do any work in India House. The management of India House needed to be wary after discovering what Kirtikar had been doing but needing a general factotum to do maintenance, shopping, and cooking, they took Tirumalachari on board. After a couple of months, it was realised that he was a genuine patriot who took an active role in the activities of India House. He was not a spy.

Useful as Tirumalachari undoubtedly was, he had to be financed by the committee who ran India House. Judging by the large amount of money Scotland Yard was paying Kirtikar for his 'fake news', it was decided to provide the police with another source of information. Aiyar persuaded Tirumalachari to visit Scotland Yard and offer his services as a paid informer, claiming that he was being exploited by the management of India House. Scotland Yard employed him. He sent the Yard information that corroborated that which Kirtikar was sending as well as harmless clippings from Indian newspapers and innocuous letters, which he claimed that he had found in the House. The ruse worked, Scotland Yard was pleased, Tirumalachari was paid, and India House received valuable funds from their cook's remuneration.

Shyamji Krishnavarma's letter published in the *Times* on the 20th of February 1909 caused a great deal of trouble. First, it led to the University of Oxford ending the scholarship, the Herbert Spencer Fellowship, that Shyamji had endowed to the university. They decided to refund his generous donation[451]. Then, on the 23rd of April 1909, the Inner Temple decided to disbar Shyamji Krishnavarma[452]. The reason given for terminating his membership of the Inner Temple related to letters published in the *Times*, notably on the 20th of February and the 10th of March, and elsewhere including the *Indian Sociologist*. Shyamji was formally disbarred on the 30th of April.

Shyamji's reaction to his disbarment was published in a letter to the *Times*. He presumed that he had been disbarred by the Benchers because:

"...*they objected to my attitude towards British rule in India. I therefore confined my remarks in my written statement ... and let them judge whether an Indian was not entitled to plead for the independence of his own country just like an Englishman, supposing Germany or France conquered England and governed it despotically ... By deciding to disbar me for the expression of my political opinions, shared and supported by many noble and high-minded Englishmen*[453] , *they* [the Benchers] *have, in my humble opinion, conferred a unique honour on me, as personally I feel the full force of the words of Horace "Dulce et decorum est pro patria mori" – it is sweet and glorious to die for one's own country.*"

He continued by pointing out the inconsistency of the behaviour of the Inns of Court:

"... *It is well known that some of the of the Boer leaders, who actually fought against the British in the late South African war, were barristers, and yet to my knowledge they have not been disbarred. Like or unlike them, I owe no allegiance to the British Government, since I was born in an Indian state the natives of which "are foreigners in the eye of the law of British India" ... and I pointed this out to the Benchers of my Inn, who evidently think that the sauce for the goose is not sauce for the gander ...*[454]"

He concluded his letter by suggesting that in view of official interference and suspicion of his India House in Highgate, he was considering closing it and opening a new one in Paris, where he was now residing.

Soon after Shyamji's disbarment, the Benchers of Grays Inn postponed calling two Indian students to the Bar[455]. The Benchers explained that they had not refused to ever call them to the Bar but wanted to delay their decision until the accusations against them had been fully investigated. Both men had been accused of being involved with revolutionary activities at India House. One of them, Veer Savarkar, who had been a manager of the House, was never called, but the other, Harnam Singh, was eventually called to the Bar[456].

Meanwhile in London, Savarkar was becoming alarmed by the public criticism of his 'guru' Shyamji. As a result, on the 3rd of April, he moved his place of residence from India House to the home of Bipin Chandra Pal at 140 Sinclair Road in Shepherds Bush. Despite his move to Shepherds Bush, Savarkar, furious about the arrest of his brother Ganesh, continued to attend meetings at India House[457]. The latter was no longer 'headed' by Savarkar but by Haider Raza. Savarkar and Raza had quarrelled over a question of the House's policy and appealed to Krishnavarma, who decided in favour of Raza. Savarkar took umbrage and resigned as leader of the House[458].

By the early months of 1909, Madan Lal Dhingra's engineering examinations at University College were over, allowing him to devote more time to activities connected with India House[459]. He had fulfilled his family's wishes and hoped to return to India later in the year. At that time, two things had influenced him greatly[460]. One was the manifesto of the Polish Revolutionary Party, which advocated armed rising and terrorism as the only way for achieving independence. The other was the arrest of Savarkar's brother Ganesh. In order to mix with and meet individuals high in British society, Madan Lal joined the National Indian Association and an aristocratic club, both in London[461]. His purpose for joining these organisations, which differed so much from India House, was sinister.

Around May 1909, Kundan Lal Dhingra, one of Madan Lal's elder brothers, wrote a letter to WH Curzon Wyllie, who was by now a senior member of the India Office. He asked Wyllie to use his influence to detach Madan Lal from his connection with India House[462]. Curzon Wyllie asked Miss Beck, Secretary of the National Indian Association, a group loyal to the British, to invite Madan Lal to participate in their activities. Madan Lal, an associate-member, was then invited to attend meetings. Wyllie also wrote to Madan Lal requesting a visit from him. Kundan Lal had also written to his brother informing him of his communication with Wyllie, but Madan Lal never replied to the British administrator's invitation.

On the 9th of June, Veer Savarkar's brother Ganesh was sentenced to transportation for life[463] to the Andaman Islands. At a regular Sunday meeting in India House, Veer was:

"…especially violent and repeated his oath to wreak his vengeance on the British …[464]*"*
He was not the only person, who promised to do so.

Madan Lal Dhingra left India House and moved into a ground floor room rented to him at 108 Ledbury Road by Mrs Mini Harris on Easter Monday (12th of April 1909). At about 2 pm on the 1st of July, he left his room and made his way to the Fairyland shooting range in Tottenham Court Road. It was here that he had been visiting two or three times a week to practice shooting with his Belgian-made[465] Browning Colt automatic pistol. He had purchased this weapon in late January from William Burrow, an employee of Gamage's Ltd, after showing a gun licence in his own name. On the 1st of July, Madan Lal was in good form. At 5.30 pm, he fired twelve shots at a target eighteen feet away and hit it eleven times. He returned to his room at Ledbury Road at about 8 pm, changed, left in a cab dressed in his usual clothes and a blue turban. He was carrying an invitation, sent by Miss Beck (see above), to an event being held by the National Indian Association at the Jehangir Hall at the Imperial Institute in South Kensington. All that remains of this institute today, which was demolished between 1957 and 1962[466] , is the impressive Queen's Tower and two weather-beaten stone lions next to it. These stand within the campus of Imperial College.

Miss Beck met Madan Lal at about 10.30 pm at the party and asked him how he was getting on with his studies. He replied that he had completed his course at University College and was planning to take the Associate Member of the Institute of Civil Engineers examinations in October before returning to India. He told her that he recognised a few of the people at the party.

At about 11 pm, Madan Lal engaged William Curzon Wyllie in conversation. Soon after beginning to speak, Madan Lal raised his arm and fired four shots into Curzon Wyllie's face, neck, and eyes. He fired two more shots, one of them killing a bystander, an Indian man in evening dress, a physician Dr Cawas Lalcaca (a Parsi born in Ahmedabad[467]), who fell backwards. He died later at the nearby St Georges Hospital. Then, Madan Lal put his revolver to his temple and squeezed the trigger. There was only a click. Whether it was intention to commit suicide rather than face a trial in which he could express his opinions publicly is uncertain. He might have put the gun to his head in the heat of the moment. Douglas Thorburn, a journalist attending the party who saw all of this, managed with the help of others nearby, including one of the other witnesses to the shooting Sir Leslie Probyn, to restrain Madan Lal and bring him to the ground.

When asked why he had shot the two men, Madan Lal did not reply but asked to be allowed to put on his spectacles. When another of the guests at the event, Captain Charles Rolleston, asked his identity and address, Madan Lal replied "Dhingra, Ledbury Road." When Rolleston, speaking mostly in Hindustani, asked Madan Lal why he had he had shot the two guests, he replied "I will tell the police."

When the police arrived at the Institute and arrested Madan Lal, they found in his pockets: the weapon used in the shooting, another revolver, a dagger, bullets, and some papers. All of these were confiscated. Madan Lal was taken to Marylebone Police Station and charged with the killings. On the next day at Westminster Police Court, just before he was remanded in custody, Madan Lal told the magistrate:
"The only thing I want to say is that there was no wilful murder in the case of Dr Lalcaca; I did not know him; when he advanced to take hold of me I simply fired in self-defence."

Madan Lal was tried for murder at the Old Bailey Court on the 19th of July 1909. When asked to plead guilty or not guilty for the murder of Curzon Wyllie, Madan Lal replied:
"First of all I would say that these words cannot be used with regard to me at all. Whatever I did was an act of patriotism and justice which was justified. The only thing I have to say is in the statement which I believe you have got…"
And then:
"Well, according to my view I will plead "Not guilty". Whatever I want to say is in the statement that was taken from my pocket."
Later, we will return to this statement taken from Madan Lal at the time of his arrest. It was of considerable importance to Madan Lal that it should be read out in court. After the statement he had made at the Marylebone Police Court, which was not the written one he carried before his arrest, was read out, Madan Lal said:

"I do not want to say anything in defence of myself, but simply to prove the justice of my deed. As for myself, no English law court has got any authority to arrest and detain me in prison, or pass sentence of death on me. That is the reason I did not have any counsel to defend me.

And I maintain that if it is patriotic in an Englishman to fight against the Germans if they were to occupy this country, it is much more justifiable and patriotic in my case to fight against the English. I hold the English people responsible for the murder of 80 millions of Indian people in the last fifty years, and they are also responsible for taking away £100,000,000 every year from India to this country. I also hold them responsible for the hanging and deportation of my patriotic countrymen, who did just the same as the English people here are advising their countrymen to do ... Just as the Germans have no right to occupy this country, so the English people have no right to occupy India, and it is perfectly justifiable on our part to kill the Englishman who is polluting our sacred land. I am surprised at the terrible hypocrisy, the farce, and the mockery of the English people. They pose as the champions of oppressed humanity—the peoples of the Congo and the people of Russia—when there is terrible oppression and horrible atrocities committed in India; for example, the killing of two millions of people every year and the outraging of our women ... Whatever else I have to say is in the paper before the Court I make this statement, not because I wish to plead for mercy or anything of that kind. I wish that English people should sentence me to death, for in that case the vengeance of my countrymen will be all the more keen. I put forward this statement to show the justice of my cause to the outside world, and especially to our sympathisers in America and Germany."

Madan Lal remained unhappy about the proceedings. When asked if he wished to present any evidence, he said:

"There is another statement on foolscap paper. It was taken from my pocket among other papers..."

This was the one taken from him at the time of his arrest, and he was unable to remember its wording. The Lord Chief Justice replied:

"I don't care what was in your pocket. The question of what you have written before has nothing to do with this case. You have got to say anything you wish to the Jury. What you have written on previous occasions or what was in your pocket is no evidence in this case. If you

wish to say anything to the Jury in defence of yourself say it now. Do you wish to say anything more?"

Madan Lal had no more to say. On hearing that he had been sentenced to death, he declared to the court:

"I have told you over and over again that I do not acknowledge the authority of the Court, You can do whatever you like. I do not mind at all. You can pass sentence of death on me. I do not care. You white people are all-powerful now, but, remember, it shall have our turn in the time to come, when we can do what we like."

As Madan Lal was being removed from the court, he added:

"Thank you, my Lord. I don't care. I am proud to have the honour of laying down my life for the cause of my motherland."

After he had been taken to the cells, Mr Tindal Atkinson KC, acting for Madan Lal's family, told the court that the family viewed his crime with greatest abhorrence and emphasised strongly that they had not the slightest sympathy with the views and motives that led to the crime, adding they were very loyal subjects of the British Empire. The Lord Chief Justice replied:

"I am very glad you should have said that on behalf of the members of the family.[468]"

Back in India, Madan Lal's brother Behari Lal wrote to his friend Sir James Dunlop on the 4th of July 1909:

"Though every man is responsible for his actions and must suffer himself, our whole family is filled with shame and deepest sorrow at Madan's act ..."

Three days later, Behari and his brother Mohan Lal added:

"... We felt the deepest agony at the mere thought of the London tragedy, for Sir Curzon Wyllie was one of our kindest friends..."

Wondering how their brother had become involved in assassination, they added that Madan Lal was:

"... discovered as an excellent tool for evil purposes by Krishnavarma and his lieutenants. He was probably given lectures and taught the use of revolvers and daggers ..."

And then, suggesting that Madan Lal was not of sound mind, they added:

"Madan Lal made an exhibition of eccentricity in London during the very first week – by cutting off the whiskers of the pet cat of the landlady of his lodgings...[469]"

Madan Lal maintained a calm, collected demeanour throughout his trial and when he was about to be executed. Winston Churchill, at that time President of The Board of Trade, was impressed by Dhingra. He could quote Dhingra's words in court from memory and wrote that they were:
"... the finest ever made in the name of patriotism..."
He predicted to his friend Wilfrid Blunt that Dhingra would be remembered for two thousand years:
"...just as we remember Regulus and Spartacus and Plutarch's heroes...[470]"

On the same day as Madan Lal's trial, Arthur Horsley was tried at the Old Bailey, charged with printing and publishing the *Indian Sociologist*, which was described as:
"...a wicked, scandalous, and seditious libel concerning the Government of the King of and ... Indian Empire and the administration of the laws in force there...[471]"
Horsley was sentenced to four months imprisonment.

Madan Lal was hanged at Pentonville Jail on Tuesday the 17th of August 1909[472]. A few weeks before that on the 22nd of July, Savarkar visited him in prison to pay his respects and to receive the blessings of the condemned 'martyr'[473]. At that meeting, Madanlal told Veer that his only last wish was to be cremated, and his corpse was not to be touched by any non-Hindu. He also asked that his clothes and other possessions be sold to raise money for the national cause[474]. Contrary to his wishes, Madan Lal's remains were buried in the grounds of Pentonville. His acts of violence at the Imperial Institute shocked the British people and marked the beginning of the rapid decline both of India House and extremist Indian nationalist activities in England.

From the earliest days of India House, its members were expected to do at least one daily deed to help India. These deeds included writing to newspapers in England and India, corresponding with sympathetic patriots all over the world, and physical activities (such as gymnastics, horse-riding, boxing, wrestling, shooting practice, car driving, etc.). The residents were also expected to keep diaries, which were inspected by the senior members of the Free India Society[475]. At India House, VVS Aiyar spent much time writing journalistic material both in English and his native Tamil. He wrote much following the Curzon-Wyllie assassination, especially to a journal, *India*, published in India. Mr Bharati, its editor, was against what Madan Lal had done, but its proprietor disagreed with him. In one of his *London letters*, published in *India*, Aiyar wrote about Madan Lal's corpse:

"Dhingra had asked the authorities to cremate the body. But they refused to accede to his last wish. While they bury the dead in England, the Hindu custom is to cremate them. All that Dhingra had asked was that his body be consigned to the flames according to his own religious practice. The authorities refused. Agni, the Lord of Fire, was ready to receive as oblation the body of this divine son of India. But, denied of this, Agni got annoyed and razed to the ground in a huge fire a cotton mill in Glasgow, swallowing material worth two lakh and fifty thousand pounds sterling. Perhaps in Agni's view, Dhingra's body was worth that much[476].

Madan Lal's family was horrified by what he had done not only tried to make out that he was insane but also dropped the name 'Dhingra' from their names[477]. When he was examined by a physician, Dr SR Dyer, in Brixton prison, it was found that Madan Lal was neither mentally subnormal nor suffering from any other mental problems; he was sane[478].

Veer Savarkar, who was away in Reading on the day of the shooting[479], learnt about the murder of Curzon Wyllie first-hand from fellow revolutionary Koregoankar who was present at the party at the Imperial Institute. Koregoankar had probably been sent to keep an eye on Madan Lal[480] and to make sure he carried out the shooting. Laughing, he related Lady Wyllie's grief on seeing her husband lying dead. Savarkar, hearing this, said:

"A wife sobs her heart out for her husband and you laugh at it! I do not trust you perhaps, I cannot.[481]"

Savarkar was right to be suspicious of this fellow member of India House.

A few days before the Wyllie shooting, Dhingra had asked his 'guru', Savarkar whether the time for martyrdom had really arrived. Savarkar answered cryptically:

"If a martyr is determined and ready, that fact by itself implies that the time for martyrdom must have come.[482]"

Prior to killing Curzon Wyllie, Madan Lal had already attempted unsuccessfully to assassinate Lord Curzon, former Viceroy of India who had been in charge when Bengal was partitioned, and Lord Morley, Secretary of State for India, who had advocated harsh measures for suppressing sedition and insurgency in India. On the 30th of June 1909, Madan Lal visited Savarkar, who handed him a nickel-plated revolver (the one found in Madan Lal's pocket at the Imperial Institute, but not used for the murders). Savarkar said to him:

"If you fail this time, don't show me your face again.[483]"

Curzon Wyllie, whom we have encountered already several times both in India and in London, was the Political Aide-de-Camp of the Secretary of State for India, a lynchpin in the administration of British India. In addition to his primary duties, he took a great deal of benevolent interest in the welfare of Indian students and he was also devoted to associations and charities that benefitted Indians[484]. However, he was opposed to Savarkar and his followers and was responsible for planting spies in India House[485]. His sudden demise was considered by many a shock and great tragedy both in the UK and India.

Four days after the assassination of Curzon Wyllie, a public meeting of Indians was held at Caxton Hall[486] to condemn Madan Lal. So many people turned up that arrangements had to be made to accommodate the 'overflow'. The meeting was chaired by His Highness the Aga Khan. Other 'worthies' present included: The Maharajah of Cooch-Behar, Sir Dinshaw Petit (father of the future wife of Mohammed Ali Jinnah), Miss Beck of the Indian National Association, and Sir MM Bhownagree. The latter proposed a resolution that those present at the meeting and all the communities of Indians both in India and Great Britain express horror and condemnation of the murders of Curzon Wyllie and Dr Lalcaca. After this had been seconded by Mr Ameer Ali, Mr Theodore Morison, a member of the Indian Council, stepped on to the stage. He was accompanied by a young Indian, Bhajan

Lal Dhingra, the younger brother of Madan Lal. Bhajan Lal, who had been brought by Madan Lal to India House on at least one occasion[487], was a student in London. Morison told the assembly that the young man had come to the meeting to publicly purge himself of all sympathy for his brother's crime. Morison said that the shy young man also supported the meeting's resolution.

When the Chairman announced that the resolution had been passed unanimously, Veer Savarkar, who was in the audience, shouted:

"No, not all!"

Thereupon, mayhem broke out. People were filled with fear as many of them knew Veer's connections with revolution and bomb-making[488]. Many shouted that he should be thrown out and a few chairs were brandished angrily. A Mr Edward Palmer[489], of mixed British and Indian ancestry, took it upon himself to:

"… plant a truly British blow between the eyes of Savarkar who had raised a chair to fell me…[490]"

Tirumal Acharya, who helped to defend Veer from further attacks by Palmer, first thrashed Palmer and then began helping his friend get away from the hall[491]. Before this, VVS Aiyar had threatened Palmer with a gun, but Veer winked at him to restrain him[492]. A few days later, Virendranath Chattopadhyaya, who was unable to attend the meeting, wrote to the London *Times*, saying that if he had been present, he would have supported Veer's objection even at the risk of being thrown out[493]. He added that although he objected to the resolution and believed in the right to express one's own opinion, he did not consider that assassination and anarchism was the right way to achieve the independence of his country.

Bipin Chandra Pal was one of the many assembled at Caxton Hall who strongly condemned Madan Lal's actions. He lived at 140 Sinclair Road in Shepherds Bush. This is where Savarkar was living at the time of Curzon Wyllie's assassination, as was pointed out by a correspondent to the *Times*[494]. When an angry crowd gathered outside, the house, Pal had to tell them that apart from being a paying guest, Veer had no other association with him[495]. Another resident at this address, Pal's son Niranjan, was a close friend of Veer's and a regular visitor to India House[496]. Niranjan's association with India House worried Bipin greatly.

Five days after Curzon Wyllie's demise, Mr Louis Allen, a member of the highly respected Reform Club of London, wrote a letter[497] to its Club Secretary suggesting removing his fellow member, Mr FC Mackarness, a Member of Parliament (for Newbury) from the Club because of his and his colleagues' alleged responsibility for the "… *seething unrest that is so dangerously rampant in our British Empire*." Mr Mackarness was the Chairman of the Executive of the India Civil Rights Committee (founded in 1908[498]). Prior to the shooting at the Imperial Institute, he had protested strongly against the trials (without juries and the right to cross-examine or even to see police witnesses) of alleged dissidents in India. For example, in late January 1909, he had written in a letter to the *Times*:

"I hardly think, Sir, that you will differ from me when I say that to apply the old East India Company regulation of 1818 to British subjects for the purpose of depriving them of their personal liberty by a mere administrative order is a violation of certain fundamental principles secured to us all by Magna Carta, and by the Habeas Corpus Act of 1679. Indeed it is a violation of a much earlier law still … It was decided in 1861 that the King's Bench had always possessed jurisdiction to serve a writ of Habeas Corpus in a proper case to any part of the King's dominions. It remains to be seen whether modern legislation, here or in India, has deprived Indians or Anglo-Indians of the right to this high prerogative writ … If it has, then the safeguards against arbitrary imprisonment in India must be brought up to the levels of those which exist in other parts of the British Empire.[499]"

Five months later, and less than a fortnight before Curzon Wyllie was shot, Mackarness wrote criticizing the questionable 'trials' of Indians arrested often without their knowledge of the charges against them:

"Lord Morley's plan … is to ignore Parliament, to act as if martial law has been declared, and to deprive the persons arrested even of that summary trial to which they would have been entitled even under martial law … Above all [the judges in India] *have not heard what the accused persons – men of untarnished record – have to say in answer to the charges secretly brought against them. We think that so to treat such men must bring not peace but sword.*[500]"

Following the shooting, Mackarness was accused of not displaying enough sympathy towards the victims. It must have been this and his desire to see that Indians received fair trial in India that had prompted Mr Allen to write to the Club Secretary. Mackarness replied to the accusation of not expressing regret for the murders that the opposite was the case:

"I took it for granted that no man in his right mind could do other than sorrow for what happened as not merely a grievous personal tragedy but a public calamity of grave significance.[501]*"*

The Reform Club decided to take no action against Mackarness. Consequently, Mr Louis Allen resigned. This episode illustrates that despite some British being either in favour of the summary 'justice' being meted out in India, there were others who objected to it.

After the assassination of Curzon Wyllie, the police thoroughly searched Dhingra's house in Ledbury Road, India House, and they ransacked the premises where the *Indian Sociologist* was printed. The press brayed for Shyamji Krishnavarma's extradition from France. Shyamji denied knowing Dhingra, who had arrived at India House, so he said, after he had left London for Paris. In a letter to the London *Times,* he wrote:

"Allow me to say at the very outset that on personal grounds I regret the death of Sir Curzon Wyllie."

After describing in detail his close and amicable relationship with Curzon Wyllie whilst working as a Diwan in India (a friendship that might have diminished after Shyamji was 'sacked' from Junagadh), he wrote[502]:

"These facts ought to convince every unbiased man that I could not have been party to the assassination of Sir Curzon Wyllie. This does not, however, prevent me from holding that, if an assassination be on political grounds, it is justifiable, but that, if it be on private or personal grounds, it is not justifiable ... I frankly admit I approve of the deed, and regard its author as a martyr to the cause of Indian independence."

After quoting from Richard Congreve, who wrote in 1857 that the British should remove themselves from India as quickly as possible and to put in motion measures to encourage the smooth commencement of Indian independence, Shyamji warned that failure to heed Congreve's advice would:

"...ere long befall England a catastrophe which will 'stagger humanity'".

Thus, in his long letter, Shyamji tried to refute any hint of personal involvement with the murder of Curzon Wyllie whilst wholeheartedly approving it.

After the murders committed by Madan Lal, India House soon closed, and its residents dispersed[503]. Before it closed, a meeting was held there on the 4th of July. Speeches praising Madan Lal were made by VVS Aiyar, Gyanchand Varma, Haider Raza, SM Master, and Savarkar. Aiyar said that Madan Lal had carried out a glorious act and hinted that there was "someone in their midst" (he was probably referring to Savarkar), who was the real creator of a man like Dhingra. He also reported that had it not been for Koregaonkar's presence at the Imperial Institute and his alertness, Curzon Wyllie might easily have left the party without Madan Lal noticing him. Dr Rajan also present at this meeting, which was being spied on by a police informer, said that Madan Lal was a product of Savarkar's sound teaching. Referring to the assassination, Savarkar said:

"It is an initial step; I have still to avenge my brother's life.[504]*"*
Veer was referring to his brother's life sentence of incarceration in the horrendous Cellular Jail on the Andaman Islands.

Savarkar moved to a room above a small Indian restaurant in Red Lion Passage (which no longer exists as it was built over with council flats either before or just after the Second World War). He shared the rooms with Sukhsagar Dutt, who had introduced the young David Garnett to Savarkar. David often visited Veer there, and wrote later:

"As a result I saw a certain amount of Savarkar and was more than ever struck by his extraordinary personal magnetism. There was an intensity of faith in the man and a curious single-minded recklessness which were deeply attractive to me. The filthy place in which he was living brought out both his refinement and also his lack of human sympathy, both characteristic of the high-caste Brahmin. The windows of the room which Dutt and Savarkar shared as a sitting-room, looked across the narrow, filthy alley of Red Lion Passage---one of the dirtiest slums in London ... He [i.e. Savarkar] was wrapped in visions. What was his vision then? I cannot say, but I believe it was that India was a volcano, which had erupted violently during the Mutiny and which could be made to erupt again...[505]*"*

Madan Lal had been carrying a statement with him in his pocket when he fired the lethal shots at the Imperial Institute. He was hoping to read this out at the trial that he knew he would follow his deadly mission, but, as already mentioned, this was removed from him at the time of his arrest. Some say that it was not written by Madan Lal but by Veer Savarkar[506]. Veer managed to find a draft of the statement, and then wanted it published. He wanted it to be printed in France and sent to the press in Europe and the USA. During a brief visit to Brighton, Veer entrusted the job of doing this to Gyanchand Varma, who carried it out successfully[507]. However, Veer also wanted it published in England. It was David Garnett who helped achieve this:

"I met Savarkar shortly afterwards, and he gave me a copy of Dhingra's statement and asked me if I could get it published. That was easy. I took my first and only journalistic scoop to Robert Lynd, then on the staff of the Daily News, and it appeared in that paper next morning. Savarkar was extremely pleased. Curiously enough, after being deprived of his statement, Dhingra had been unable to express himself nearly so well or quite to the same effect. It occurred to me that someone might have written it for him and that he had not bothered to learn it by heart. If so, I guessed who the author of it was and realized that he was an accessory.[508]"

The contents of this statement have been reproduced many times[509], often with slight variations in its wording:

"I admit the other day; I attempted to shed English blood as an humble revenge for the inhuman hangings and deportations of patriotic Indian youths. In this attempt, I have consulted none but my own conscience; I have conspired with none, but my own duty.

I believe that a nation held down in bondage with the help of foreign bayonets is in a perpetual state of war. Since open battle is rendered impossible to a disarmed race, I attacked by surprise; since guns were denied to me, I drew forth my pistol and fired.

As a Hindu I felt that a wrong done to my country is an insult to God. Her cause is the cause of Sri Ram! Her services are the services of Sri Krishna! Poor in health and intellect, a son like myself has nothing else to offer to the Mother but his own blood and so I have sacrificed the same on her altar.

The only lesson required in India at present is to learn how to die and the only way to teach it, is by dying ourselves. Therefore I die and glory in my martyrdom! This war of Independence will continue between India and England, so long as the Hindu and the English races last (if the present unnatural relation does not cease!)

My only prayer to God is: May I be reborn of the same Mother and may I re-die in the same sacred cause, till the cause is successful and she stands free for the good of humanity and the glory of God! Vande Mataram![510]"

In the middle of July, Shyamji Krishnavarma visited London briefly and stayed with Nitisen Dwarkadas at his home in Holland Park Avenue. He had come to see India House, which he found to be in a filthy state. He had it cleaned as he was considering selling it. Soon after his return to Paris, Gyanchand Varma left London for the same destination. He was followed by Govind Amin, who had introduced men at India House to the shooting range in Tottenham Court Road. He stopped in Paris on his way back to India[511].

On the 21st of July, Koregaonkar, who had been present with Dhingra at the Imperial Institute, was guest of honour at a farewell dinner held at the Indian restaurant at Red Lion Passage. All the prominent members of India House were present. Savarkar chaired the proceedings which were partly to thank Koregaonkar for his work in helping Indian nationalism. Three days later, having paid Dhingra a visit in prison, Koregaonkar left for India on the *SS Austria*, arriving in Bombay on the 18th of August. According to the city's Commissioner of Police, Koregaonkar told the authorities all he knew about India House. He alleged that Savarkar had shown no signs of displeasure following the murder of Curzon Wyllie[512].

MK Gandhi, who was visiting London in August 1909 on business connected with the plight of Indians in the Transvaal[513], did not approve of what Madan Lal had done or said afterwards. He wrote in *Indian Opinion*:

"It is being said in defence of Sir Curzon Wyllie's assassination that it is the British who are responsible for India's ruin, and that, just as the British would kill every German if Germany invaded Britain, so too it is the right of any Indian to kill any Englishman. Every Indian should reflect thoughtfully on this murder. It has done India much harm: the deputation's efforts have also received a setback. But that

need not be taken into consideration. It is the ultimate result that we must think of. Mr. Dhingra's defence is inadmissible. In my view, he has acted like a coward. All the same, one can only pity the man. He was egged on to do this act by ill digested reading of worthless writings. His defence of himself, too, appears to have been learnt by rote. It is those who incited him to this that deserve to be punished. In my view, Mr. Dhingra himself is innocent. The murder was committed in a state of intoxication. It is not merely wine or bhang that makes one drunk; a mad idea also can do so.[514]"

Whether Madan Lal was intoxicated with alcohol or bhang[515], rather than a 'mad idea', when he set out to kill Curzon Wyllie or not known. The police, who arrested him and the medical people who examined him subsequently did not record any signs of chemical intoxication.

For a while after Dhingra's hanging on the 17th of August 1909, Sunday meetings were still being held at India House[516], but also elsewhere. In October, the festival of Dussehra was celebrated at Nizam-u-Din's restaurant, The Indian Catering Company, at 36 Ledbury Road in Bayswater[517]. Gandhi had been invited to chair the proceedings. He had accepted the invitation on condition that the food would be pure vegetarian and that discussion of controversial politics was avoided. The food was served by Savarkar's followers: VVS Aiyar, Tirimul Acharya, and TSS Rajan[518], all sometime members of India House.

The festival of Dussehra commemorates the rescue of Rama's queen Sita and his victory over her abductor the devil Ravana. Gandhi gave a speech in which he spoke of Rama's suffering in exile, Sita's remaining pure despite undergoing suffering, and her brother practising austerity. He concluded that it was such personal sacrifices that would deliver India's freedom and would show that truth conquers falsehood. His speech was followed by that of Veer Savarkar, who also used tales from the *Ramayana* to camouflage his underlying message. He emphasised the role of the goddess Durga, the avenger. Also, he pointed out that Rama only achieved his ideal kingdom after slaying Ravana, the symbol of oppression and injustice. Thus, while Gandhi was using mythology to promote peaceful means of achieving independence, Savarkar was making the point that non-violence alone would be ineffective without using violent methods[519]. On his return to South

Africa in November on the *Kildonan Castle*, Gandhi wrote his *Hind Swaraj*, which is to some extent his literary response to the violent revolutionaries, whom he had met in London. Parel, who has produced a scholarly annotated edition of *Hind Swaraj*, noted:

"It is difficult to estimate the extent of Savarkar's role in the formulation of the philosophy of Hind Swaraj: D Keer, the biographer of both Gandhi and Savarkar, goes so far as to claim that it was written in response to Savarkar. This is clearly an exaggeration, but there is definitely some truth in it. [520]"

It is fair to say that some of the roots of this widely read work sprung from its author's encounters with India House and its members.

Savarkar had been asked to leave BC Pal's home after it had been stoned by a mob[521]. It was then that he moved into the rooms above the Indian restaurant in the slum-like red Lion Passage along with Sukhsagar Dutt who had quarrelled with BC Pal. During the last two months of 1909, Savarkar suffered from physical (fever and bronchitis) and psychological (mental stress) problems[522].

India House, which had been under intense police surveillance since the shootings at the Imperial Institute, was closed by the police. In late summer, Shyamji Krishnavarma's wife Bhanumati visited London for three weeks to arrange the sale of India House[523]. The sale took a long time. It remained empty and unsold for a long time and was still on the market in February 1910, when a report in the *Times* noted that Shyamji was prepared to gift of the House to the Indian nation on condition that it was used as residential quarters and a meeting place for discussing and disseminating views on the independence of India[524]. This did not happen.

With the closure of India House as a student hostel following Madan Lal's arrest, Indian revolutionary activity in London began to peter out. The next chapter will describe the last few months in Europe of India House's most famous resident, and then the following one deals with the last years of Shyamji Krishnavarma.

VICTORIA STATION TO PORT BLAIR

On the 10th of December 1909, Veer Savarkar, who was exhausted after numerous secret meetings and evading detectives, visited Brighton with BC Pal's son Niranjan Pal. Sitting by the beach feeling homesick, Veer wrote a plaintive poem:

> *"Take me O Ocean!*
> *Take me to my native shores.*
> *Thou promised me to take me to my native home.*
> *But the coward,*
> *Afraid of thy mighty master,*
> *Britain, thou hast betrayed me.*
> *But mind my mother is not altogether helpless.*
> *She will complain to Sage Agasti*
> *And in a draught he will swallow thee as he did in the past*[525]"

This poem, which probably sounds better in its original Marathi, was well-received by the *literati* of Maharashtra.

News from Nasik just before Christmas made Savarkar question the wisdom of remaining in England. On the 22nd of December 1909, Mr AMT Jackson, the Collector of Nasik, was shot dead by a young Indian as he was about to attend a performance in the city's Vijayanand Theatre[526]. His murderer, eighteen-year-old Anananta Laxman Kanare, a Chitpavan Brahmin, was captured with his Browning revolver as he tried to shoot himself. He told his captors that he had travelled from Aurangabad with the specific purpose of killing Jackson. Repeatedly, he told them that he had shot Jackson to avenge the recent sentencing of Veer's brother Ganesh[527].

Numerous arrests were made following the murder because the authorities suspected that the killing was part of a conspiracy. Most of those arrested were, like Kanare and the Savarkars, Chitpavan

Brahmins. Amongst them, there were three members of the Public Works Department, in whose houses revolvers and ammunition were found. Veer Savarkar's younger brother Narayan was also arrested and sentenced to six months imprisonment. He was already a suspect in the case of the bombs, which had been thrown at the Viceroy and Lady Minto outside the Rani Sipri Mosque in Ahmedabad on the 13th of November[528]. The bombs used were coconuts filled with picric acid[529], a chemical with which Veer had been experimenting at India House.

Commenting on the murder, Shyamji Krishnavarma writing (using the 'royal we') in Paris commented:

"Oddly enough, we knew Mr. Jackson personally just as we did Sir Curzon Wyllie, who was assassinated last July It was at Oxford that we met Mr. Jackson last. He was a pupil of the present Boden Professor of Sanskrit, Dr. A. A. MacDonald, who in his turn was a pupil of ours for nearly five years in our old Oxford days [530]*."*

Also, Shyamji emphasised:

"...that we had absolutely nothing to do directly or indirectly with the assassination in question, in which our calumniators have been endeavouring so carefully to implicate us."

Shyamji was referring to reports in the press that implied connections with people inspired by him and the shooting. Despite emphasising that he had no hand in the murder or its planning, Shyamji wrote that he regarded Kanare as a 'martyr'. Also, he announced two new scholarships:

"...as our tribute to the noble examples set by Mr. Hema Chandra Das and Mr. Ganesh Savarkar, who have been recently sentenced to transportation for life at the instance of the foreign oppressors of India.[531]*"*

The London *Times* writing about the murder of Jackson and the Chitpavan Brahmins, whose members included the great nationalist Tilak, noted:

"These unpleasant facts bear out only too fully ... the grave significance of the part played by that powerful caste in the propaganda of Indian disaffection.[532]*"*

The Browning pistol with which Kanare had shot Jackson was, it was later discovered, one that had been sent to India from England by Veer Savarkar. It was one of a batch of twenty-one that Chatturbhuj Amin had smuggled into India in the false bottom of his baggage[533]. Later, under torture, Amin attributed all the violent acts (Curzon Wyllie, Jackson, and others) to the Savarkar brothers. He added that the weapons, including that used by Dhingra, were supplied by Savarkar. The police discovered that the weapons recovered in India were traceable to a French firm, which had been used by the nationalist revolutionaries[534].

Suspecting that information like this might come to light, an emergency meeting of the London branch of Abhinav Bharat was held. It was decided that it would be best for Veer to leave London for Paris. Across the Channel in France, Shyamji Krishnavarma and Madame Cama in Paris held the same opinion[535] and advised him to join them there. So, on about the 5th of January 1910, Veer, having recovered from pneumonia, headed out of London. Before his departure from Victoria Station, he ate a final meal of rice and grams prepared at Nizam-ud-Din's restaurant[536].

In Paris, Veer stayed at the home of Madame Cama, a valiant worker for the cause of freeing India from the British. During his stay in Paris, he had discussions and held meetings to continue his propaganda work. He used to take regular walks and rested in the gardens of Paris to improve his health[537]. However, something happened in Bombay that was soon to lead Savarkar into deep trouble.

On the 17th of January 1910, following an order by George Clarke, the Governor of Bombay, a complaint was filed against Veer by the Special Magistrate of Nasik, Mr Montgomerie[538]. A telegraphic arrest warrant was issued and sent to London by the Bombay Government acting within the provisions of the Fugitive Offenders Act of 1881[539], which dealt with the return of fugitives from one part of the British Empire to another. The charges against Veer were:

"Waging war or abetting the waging of war against His Majesty the King Emperor of India; Conspiring to deprive His Majesty the King of the Sovereignty of British India or a part of it; Procuring and distributing arms and abetting the murder of Jackson; Procuring and distributing arms in London and waging war from London; and Delivering seditious speeches in India from January to March 1906 and in London from 1908 to 1909[540]."

However, Veer was in Paris, outside the British Empire and out of the reach of the British and Indian police. He was all for returning to London to face the charges, but his friends tried to dissuade him. Shyamji Krishnavarma, who saw him frequently in Paris, wrote some time later:

"A few months ago, much against our earnest advice, he took it into his head to return to England ... On the last occasion when we met him he promised that he would have another interview with us before leaving Paris; but as fate would have it he quitted France on Sunday, the 13th of March, having penned the previous day a few lines expressing his sorrow that he could not see us and thanking us heartily for all our kindness to him, as he generously put it.[541]*"*

Veer felt that he would be safe in London just as it had been for exiles such as Orsini (who tried to kill Napoleon III) and Karl Marx[542]. But as Padmanabhan, a biographer of VVS Aiyar wrote, Veer:

"... forgot that the British treatment of fellow white men was different from their treatment of brown Indians on whose wealth the Empire was fattening.[543]*"*

Furthermore, Veer felt that it was immoral that he was enjoying a pleasant life in Paris whilst his comrades and followers were rotting in jail in India, or worse. After all, as he told VVS Aiyar who was visiting Paris on some confidential business, he had spent years preaching that it was the right thing to face, arrest, torture, jail, or even death for the freedom of India, and now it was his turn to do so[544]. When asked by Niranjal Pal why he had ignored his friends' advice not to return to England, Veer, who was by then in prison, answered that his shoulders were broad enough to bear the consequences[545].

On the 13th of March 1909, Veer was arrested on the platform at Victoria Station, having just crossed the English Channel. The following day, he appeared at Bow Street Police Court and was charged *"on a Provisional Warrant issued under the Fugitive Offenders Act*[546]*"*. Veer gave his address as Upper Addison Gardens, West Kensington. He was charged with 'sedition' as well as 'abetment of murder in India'. During the hearing, it was noted that Veer had been under Scotland Yard's surveillance for quite some time and that the details of his offences were still awaiting arrival from India. Mr Reginald Vaughan, who was employed by VVS Aiyar to defend Veer, asked for bail[547]. He pointed out that Veer had known that he had been under the eye of Scotland Yard for quite a long period and had made no attempt to leave the country. And, when he did leave for Paris, he returned to London. Bail was refused until the judge, Sir Albert de Rutzen, knew more about the case. Then, Veer was incarcerated at Brixton Prison[548].

Veer remained in Brixton Prison for several weeks, awaiting the arrival from India of the charges against him. Various friends including VVS Aiyar and David Garnett visited him regularly. Once a week, he was driven to the court at Bow Street in a taxi with two guards. Each time, bail was refused, and he would be remanded in custody for yet another week[549]. Savarkar hoped (against hope, I imagine) that he would be tried in England where sentencing would be more lenient than that imposed by courts in India.

On the 23rd of April 1910[550], Veer appeared in court again. This time it was to hear the charges, which had arrived from India, being read out. Veer was defended by an eminent Indian barrister Mr Jethalal M Parikh (born in Ahmedabad). He was a member of the Middle Temple and was called to the Bar in 1895[551]. He had been present along with other Indian 'worthies' at the inauguration of India House in 1905. When Tilak attempted to appeal against three of his convictions in early 1909, Parikh was one of the three barristers representing him[552]. In November 1909, the London *Times* reported Parikh had chaired a meeting of the London Indian Society, at which some men had proposed resolutions to express their disapproval of the 'anarchist' movement and the use of force. As chairman, Parikh said he would not allow these resolutions to be considered[553]. Another incident at that meeting, which had been inaccurately reported in the Times, had, so Parikh wrote in a letter to the paper[554], led to his resignation from the Society. However, he had condemned the actions of Madan Lal Dhingra[555] Despite his efforts, Veer remained in prison. Along with the arrival of the papers from India came the discovery that they contained the sworn testimony:

" *... of Harischandra Korgaonkar, who was an enthusiastic member of the Free India Society and India House in 1908-9, betraying the secrets of the India House patriots. In a 120-typed page statement, Korgaonkar who had turned approver, threw all blame on Savarkar* *and Aiyar for enticing Indian students in England into the path of revolution ..."*

They also revealed that there was another deposition, namely:

"Chencheri Rama Rao, who had come from Rangoon to London for higher studies in sanitary engineering. He had stated that it was Savarkar who had given him some revolvers to take to India.[556]"

This was untrue, as it was VVS Aiyar who had given Rao the weapons, which the customs found in his baggage in Bombay, in Paris. Rama Rao broke down in police custody in India after the police had discovered amongst his belongings a box with a false bottom containing an automatic pistol with eighty rounds of ammunition and several copies of Veer's book on the 1857 rebellion[557]. The police in India made Rama Rao swear that these illegal imports were not supplied by Aiyar but by Veer, against whom they were desperately trying to frame a case. In exchange for his 'cooperation', his betrayal and lying, Rama Rao was pardoned and given a job in the Indian Police Department[558].

In late May, JM Parikh and Mr KA Powell KC, a senior barrister, put in a plea for Habeas Corpus on behalf of Veer, following his committal for removal to India by Sir Albert de Rutzen. They were asking for him to be presented to the court. Nothing resulted from this hearing [559]. Veer's case was heard again, this time in the High Court of Justice, on the 2nd of June[560]. A strong defence was made by Mr Powell and Mr Parikh, but no decision was reached that day. Veer remained incarcerated. In early June at another court hearing, it was revealed that under the Indian Criminal Law Amendment Act of 1908, if Veer was returned to India for trial, he would face a tribunal of three judges without a jury[561]. The appeal for Habeas Corpus was finally quashed in the Court of Appeal on the 17th of June[562], making it increasingly likely that Veer was to be sent to India to face trial.

By the 21st of June, Veer felt certain about his fate. In a letter to VVS Aiyar (addressing him as 'Rishi') from Brixton, he wrote:

"The case does not seem to end today. Of course, both of us know the result already. Tomorrow the formal result will be given. By this time. My dear Rishi, I have got quite used to the food and mode of living here It was good that I did not ask for special food from the beginning. Now to make me a full-fledged life transportee, only a change of clothes is wanting. [563]"

At the time he received this letter, Aiyar was ready to be called to the Bar. Unwilling to swear loyalty to the king when he was called, he decided to resign from Lincolns Inn and to forego becoming a barrister[564] in order to serve his country in its struggle for freedom.

During his long stay in Brixton Prison, Veer was visited by Indian revolutionaries from both England and France[565]. Various plans were made to help him escape from Brixton, but none succeeded. Fearing that Aiyar might try to organise Veer's escape while he was being moved to India, a warrant was issued for his arrest. Aiyar managed to avoid capture by changing his place of residence frequently. The police suspected that he would try to escape to France or Brazil, but the wily Aiyar, a South Indian Brahmin, fooled them by fleeing to Holland disguised as a Sikh. From Amsterdam, he moved to Paris[566].

VVS Aiyar (from Wikipedia)

On the 29th of June, Winston Churchill, then Secretary of State for Home affairs, issued an order that Veer should be taken in custody to India[567]. He was put on board the P&O vessel *SS Morea* on the 1st of July 1910 at Gravesend. He was in the custody of a Detective-Inspector from Scotland Yard and three Indian police officials[568]. On board, he was guarded by about twelve British police officers from both London and Bombay. The British Government informed the French Government that the *Morea* was heading for Bombay with an important political prisoner and if the boat should stop at Marseilles, the French police should guard against any escape attempt that Veer might make. The Chief of Police agreed to help[569].

On the 7th of July, the *SS Morea* developed engine trouble and made a longer than usual stop in the port of Marseilles. Before departing from London, Veer had written to his friends in Paris that he believed his ship was scheduled to make a stop in that southern French port. Madame Cama, along with Shyamji Krishnavarma and VVS Aiyar, hurried down to Marseilles in order to be there when the *Morea* docked[570]. According to the former publisher of *Indian Sociologist* Guy Aldred:

"When the vessel was lying alongside the wharf at Marseilles — on its way out — Savarkar went to the bathroom and while his jailors waited outside, he succeeded, after divesting himself of his clothing, in squeezing through the porthole of the ship. Swimming ashore he reached the quay and ran. Two marine gendarmes gave chase, captured the fugitive after he had gone more than three hundred metres on French soil ... This occurred on Friday, July 8th [571]"

All might have gone well for Veer had he been kept in custody by the French police. He would have been protected from the British by being held in France. The British would have had to sue for his extradition from France in the French courts, and that might have been a lengthy procedure without any certainty of its outcome. However, this did not happen. It was prevented by the arrival of British officers from the ship, who were:

"...shouting the ignoble lie "Thief, Thief" — that his semi-nude appearance rendered this charge plausible in the eyes of the French gendarmes, who presently came on the scene — that Vinayak could not utter a syllabic in French to explain that he was a political fugitive — and that it was under this deceptive impression caused by the British agents that Vinayak was arrested by the French gendarmes and turned over to the authorities of the ship.[572]"

The British officers chasing him might have bribed the French policeman to hand over Veer into their custody[573]. In any case, British policemen, by arresting him on foreign soil, had broken international law. Madame Cama and VVS Aiyar, who were coming to Marseilles to meet Veer, hoping that he might have jumped ship, arrived at the port a few hours too late to be of any use to him[574].

Veer was returned to the *Morea* and kept in much more secure confinement than before. At Aden, he was transferred to the *SS Sasti*, which carried him to Bombay[575]. Meanwhile, back in Europe, snatching Veer from the French police caused an uproar, especially in France. He had been caught by French policemen and was a political prisoner. As such, he was entitled to apply for political asylum[576], but was deprived of this right by the lies that the British used to get the French policeman to release him into their custody. International law had been breached[577]

When news of Veer's arrest by the British on French soil became widely known three days after the *Morea* had left Marseilles, there was outrage in France especially amongst left-wing politicians. The socialist paper *l'Humanité* wrote:

"This abominable violation of the right of asylum was effected in absolute secrecy; had it not been for a telegram published yesterday (July 11th) in the Paris Daily Mail we should still have been in ignorance of the incident. But it is quite impossible that the matter can be allowed to rest there. In delivering up a political refugee the Marseilles authorities — admitting that they had acted on their own initiative — have committed an outrage of which account will most assuredly be demanded and in respect of which the sanction of the State itself is necessary[578]."

In France, Madame Cama, Shyamji Krishnavarma, and Mr Rana, the leaders of the Indian revolutionaries in Paris, took up Veer's case with influential politicians including the Socialist Jean Jaurés. In London, Guy Aldred, who had completed his prison sentence, fought for Veer. The French Government approached Britain for the return of Veer to French soil in order to consider his case for receiving political asylum. Britain did not return Veer but agreed to refer his case to the Hague Tribunal[579]. By the time that the Tribunal was ready to examine Veer's case, his trial in India was already underway. On the 7th of October 1910, *l'Humanité* reported:

"If the trial proceedings currently underway in India establish the guilt of Savarkar, the conviction against the Hindu will not be executed pending the decision of the arbitral tribunal. Meanwhile, Savarkar will not be released[580].

There were five members of the Hague Tribunal: an Englishman, a Frenchman, a Belgian, a Dutchman, and a Norwegian. Veer chose Jean Laurent-Frederick Longuet to represent his interests at the trial at the Hague[581]. Longuet (1876–1938) was a French Socialist and grandson of Karl Marx[582]. Longuet pointed out during his lengthy presentation to the tribunal:

"Shortly after the death of Mr. Jackson proceedings were decided against Savarkar, at the end of December 1909. He was then at Paris. The British government knew this perfectly. BUT IT MAKES NO EXTRADITION REQUEST FOR SAVARKAR, knowing full well it would have no chance of it being granted by the French government. The young writer remained four months in Paris without the authorities giving any signs of life. Only on his return to London in March 1910, was he arrested when he landed at Victoria Station ..."

Later, Longuet pointed out:

"There was no formal call from the British police to the French police, nor was there a formal surrender of the prisoner by the gendarme. In fact, as the facts are presented, it appears that the British police actually took him by force from the custody of French police officer in which he was placed, which was equivalent to a criminal abduction and arbitrary detention in the French territory

... Since, Damodar Savarkar, pursued for political offenses, was on French soil, it is apparent that first of all, he should have been entrusted to a French magistrate, better informed about the thorny issues of international law than the police. They did not think of it, it seems, and from there arose the incident

... English authorities, however, contended at first that the arrest was made entirely by the French coastguard. Anglo-Hindu police had only taken delivery of the prisoner returned on board by the French police. It does not seem, however, that the British government can hold on to this version, which contradicts all the evidence collected. The Indian police on the Morea, have since, themselves, destroyed the interpretation of the facts in the official account they gave of the incident wherein they strongly emphasize the part they had played in the arrest of Savarkar. [583]*"*

The tribunal judged in favour of Great Britain and against the return of Veer to France. It admitted that there had been an irregularity in the handing over of Veer to the British in Marseilles but there had been no breach of any known rule of international law[584]. There were many critics of this decision including the Berlin *Post* which wrote:

"We have never thought much of The Hague Court of Arbitration, that is of its impartiality and objective love of justice ... It has passed over the real issue of the Savarkar case in complete silence – namely, the fact that a political offender, who in a foreign harbour had escaped

... and had been recaptured ... was forthwith, without even the appearance of formal proceedings, handed back to the English ship. That is a crass breach of international law, and a proof of how far the subservience to England (die englischer Gefolgschaft) has brought proud France. [585]"

By the time in late February 1911 that the tribunal in the Hague had made up its mind over Veer, another court many thousands of miles away, had also come to a conclusion. Veer Savarkar wearing his prisoner identity number '32778' received news of the (Bombay) tribunal's deliberations in a cell in the Dongri Jail[586] in Bombay. Veer had been one of the thirty-eight prisoners in the dock in the Nasik Conspiracy case that began in September 1910[587]. Of these prisoners all but two were, like Savarkar, Chitpavan Brahmins[588]. During this case, Veer's counsel had applied for an adjournment to allow Veer to appeal to the British and French governments about the international incident that had arisen in Marseilles, but this application was turned down[589]. Veer was sentenced by the court (actually, it was a tribunal without a jury) in Bombay to transportation for life and forfeiture of his property[590]

Veer was moved from Dongri jail to another in Bombay at Byculla, and then to Thana jail. When one of his jailers taunted him with the comment that he would be set free in 1960, Veer silenced him by asking him:

"But is the British rule itself going to last for fifty years more?[591]"

In June 1911, Veer was taken by train to Madras. He was put on board the steamship *Maharaja*, which docked at Port Blair in the Andaman Islands on the 4th of July 1911. Soon, he passed through the portals of the infamous Cellular Jail, where one of the European jailers, an Irishman called Barrie, reminded Veer that Port Blair was not Marseilles[592].

Veer Savarkar was released early from his life-sentence in the horrendous Cellular Jail in Port Blair and other prisons. His premature release from Port Blair was due to many factors including official questioning of the suitability of the Andamans as a place of confinement for political prisoners. Between 1924, when this former leader of India House was released from jail, and the late 1930s, Veer was ordered to live in internal exile in the district of Ratnagiri and to desist from political activity. During this time, Veer wrote a book, *The Essentials of Hindutva*[593]. Veer based this book on many sources including the writings of Giuseppe Mazzini, which he read soon after he arrived at India House in 1906. Since Veer's time the meaning of Hindutva has morphed considerably and continues to do so[594].

PARIS AND GENEVA

Between 1907, when he moved from London to reside in Paris and putting India House up for sale, Shyamji Krishnavarma, along with Madame Cama and Mr Rana, was at the centre of radical Indian nationalist activities on the European mainland. Shyamji continued to create and finance new travelling fellowships for Indian scholars, but this and his taking refuge in Paris began to attract criticism. His biographer Yagnik wrote:

"Criticism had been naturally piling thick on such intermittent announcements of donations — which were said to have been designed by Shyamaji to earn cheap notoriety and cover himself with something of the martyr's halo...[595]*"*

He was also criticised for other reasons. Lala Lajpat Rai wrote:

"He has an imperious disposition and recognises no man's right to differ from him. He not only himself firmly adheres to his opinions but expects that others should have no opinions of their own at all ... In short he is a thorough autocrat ... Besides this Shyamji is very miserly. If he helps a man he expects him to remain his bondsman all his life. He is a very exacting task master. He is simply incapable of making any allowance for another man's point of view. God has made his disposition like that[596]*."*

In mitigation, Rai added: *"I have always regarded his patriotism beyond doubt. His political principles are sound to a large extent and he means well by his country*[597]*"*

Despite being criticised by fellow Indians, Shyamji devoted much time to international aspects of nationalist revolution, especially with the struggles of the Irish, Turkish, Egyptian, and later also the Chinese and Siamese nationalists. He was also in contact with the Americans, whom he tried to dissuade from making an alliance with Great Britain against the Germans in 1910. He wrote a letter to President William Taft of the USA which contained comments such as:

"A solemn pact with that arch robber and enslaver of nations, England which, I observe with some amusement, you style 'the mother country' ... Indeed your present truckling attitude towards England is enough to make the bones of your great predecessor, the first President of the United States, rattle in his coffin. Your proposed alliance with England is nothing short of putting premium on slavery as much as Americans, who themselves threw off the yoke of England will be forthwith invited to assist England in its nefarious work of holding in servitude a country whose inhabitants are animated by the same desire for freedom from tyranny and oppression as were your own people in days gone by[598]"

GL Varma claims that this letter persuaded the US Senate to turn down the proposed alliance treaty. Maybe it did help a bit, but at that time the Senate was also opposed to several other treaties that Taft had proposed[599]

Although Shyamji claimed no personal responsibility for the political assassinations in London and India, he supported them in theory[600]. He encouraged Indian nationalists to risk becoming martyrs by carrying out murders and throwing bombs. Virerendranath Chattopadhyay made a scathing comment about Shyamji at the end of a letter he wrote to the Times in March 1909, which criticised the use of political assassination:

"... I do not subscribe to Mr Krishnavarma's present politics. The day I feel convinced of the necessity of political assassination and underground work I shall cease to write. I shall return to my country and put my theories into practice. But I shall certainly not seek a safe retreat within the hospitable walls of a European city.[601]"

Back in London during the last months of the meetings at India House, its regular attenders made fun of Shyamji in his absence[602]. Furthermore, his lame reaction to the Savarkar incident in France and its consequences did his reputation no good amongst the revolutionaries in England and elsewhere[603].

By the beginning of 1911, Shyamji's influence on Indian revolutionaries began to decline. Nationalist newspapers such as *The Talwar* (edited by V Chattopadhyaya) and *Bande Mataram* (edited by Madame Cama and Har Dayal) had been publishing articles that attacked him either directly or indirectly[604]. Madame Cama, who founded the *Bande Mataram* paper, became dissatisfied with Shyamji's performance as the leader of the revolutionary Indian nationalist movement and rallied the younger revolutionaries in Paris around herself and away from Shyamji[605]. In addition, Shyamji quarrelled with Rana. On the 21st of September 1910, Shyamji attended an evening event in Paris about Egypt's problems. The other Indians present avoided Shyamji as a result of a disagreement with Madame Cama[606].

Shyamji began being criticised by people in India, who accused him of taking an easy path whilst others, following his advice, risked their lives. For example, in April 1910, he received a letter from India which said:

"You are daily referred to with scorn and contempt by writers in the English press who regard you as a contemptible coward, and this opinion is covering our cause with shame. For this reason a few of us met at Poona some time ago and took an oath to kill you at the first opportunity and so remove a stumbling block to our cause and a reflection upon the courage of the Indian nation…[607]"

A pro-British newspaper called *The Pioneer* revealed much about Shyamji's lifestyle in Paris and why young Indians fighting bravely for independence might have been critical of his encouraging them to undertake perilous activities:

"He lives in one of the finest houses in the most beautiful city in the world, and this house is situated in the most fashionable quarter of that city … It is a very elegant building … equipped with the latest improvements, electric lift, electric light, hot and cold baths and steam heated. The rooms are sumptuous and the views from the windows are magnificent; here in the midst of all the good that God has given to man, this suffering saint receives his lieutenants and satellites on Sunday afternoons. Most of them are attracted to his house by the very excellent tea and cakes and fruit which are served in abundance, and it is at these parties that the Pundit sheds crocodile tears over the famine-stricken millions of India. It is at these gatherings that he enjoins his guests to give up all worldly pleasures and live an austere life. National songs are sung, and the hated Feringhee is damned by one and all.[608]"
The paper continued by saying:

"… the editor of The Indian Sociologist is not a patriot at all, but a hypocrite who is playing with the subject for the sake of notoriety…"

Sadly, for Shyamji, this unfair criticism voiced by a pro-British journalist was shared by many of the younger Indian revolutionaries. Shyamji, who was in his early fifties in 1910, answered the suggestions of his apparent lack of bravery by claiming ill-health. He wrote:

"We should never dream of instigating or urging others to do anything which we hesitate to do ourselves ... Often owing to failing health, advancing years, temperament or some other special circumstance, one is unable to accomplish a certain task, but none the less one can admire those who, more favourably situated, have the capacity and the opportunity to perform it.[609]*"*

By 1911, Shyamji had become marginalised by his peers and former followers[610]. This did not put an end to his political activities. In March of that year, he wrote an article about unrest in India in the German magazine *Die Zeitschrift*. Yagnik claims that this article was the precursor to an alliance between Indian revolutionaries and the Germans during the First World War[611]. In June 1912, Shyamji joined of the newly formed 'International pro-India Committee' in Zurich and chaired by Champak Raman Pillai, a Tamil from Travancore. It provided anti-British articles to the German and Swiss press. Later, Pillai and others including Virendranath Chattopadhyay worked with the Germans in the First World War, sending propaganda and arms to nationalists in India[612].

When Har Dayal, who had been active at India House, arrived in Marseilles in August 1914, having broken bail in the USA where he had been arrested earlier in the year for organising Indian revolutionary activities, many of his Indian friends met him at the port. Shyamji wrote to Har Dayal from Switzerland (see below) offering him money and assistance to allow him to continue his revolutionary work. Har Dayal turned down the offer, saying that his differences with Shyamji were irreconcilable[613]. This is yet more evidence that Shyamji was out of favour with his former followers.

Even if his former Indian followers had side-lined him, Shyamji still attracted praise from other quarters including Egyptian nationalists, whose articles he published in the *Indian Sociologist*. In late September 1912, the Russian writer Maxim Gorky, who thought highly of Shyamji, wrote to him from Capri:

"I thank you heartily for sending me The Indian Sociologist and shake warmly your hand, the hand of an untiring wrestler for the liberty of the Great India, for the liberty of the Indian people ... Can I ask you to write an article for The Russian Review an article that could give to the Russian Democracy the knowledge of the Indian movement for liberty and justice? ... You, Krishnavarma, the Mazzini of India, you know the desires of your great people and you will certainly understand what the Russian people must know about the life of contemporary India.[614]"

Shyamji and his wife shifted from Paris to Geneva in Switzerland in late April 1914 because he was asked to do so by the French authorities, who did not want him in France during a state visit of the British King George V. As it happened, he had already applied for permission to live in Switzerland before this[615]. This was because he feared possible arrest by the French, who were by then allies of the British. He justified his move to Switzerland to his many critics as by referring to a Sanskrit text follows:

"Patanjali, the founder of yoga philosophy, advises all thinkers, intent on the promotion of human welfare, to avoid rousing animosity so that they may be able to carry out their projects unmolested, and in removing from Paris we are only acting up to the wise suggestion made by that ancient Indian philosopher[616]"

The First World War broke out in August 1914, by which time Shyamji was living comfortably in a five bedroom flat on the Avenue Vollande in Geneva with his wife and a few servants[617]. Because of the Swiss Government's desire to maintain neutrality during the war, there was censorship of the press, which Shyamji respected. Consequently, during the war years, the *Indian Sociologist* was not published. In addition, he felt that as a political refugee seeking sanctuary in Switzerland it would not be right to do anything to compromise the safety of the country providing him with refuge. During the War, the German authorities considered recruiting Shyamji to act against the British, but Chattopadhya warned them against the idea[618]. While he was constrained by the Swiss censorship rules, Shyamji considered writing a book about the rise of Indian nationalism, which he hoped to publish when hostilities were over. This was never written. The victory

of Britain and its allies dampened his inspiration and inclination to write[619]
.

Although the way the First World War ended, with the victory of the British, dashed his hopes for ever seeing an independent India, he did not give up working for it. He pinned his hopes on President Woodrow Wilson of the USA, who promised freedoms for nationalities and no annexations of territory. On the 8th of February 1919, Shyamji, who always generously offered his wealth to help causes he believed in, wrote to Wilson:

"In view of the establishment of your proposed League of Nations and in honour of your most welcome visit to Europe I respectfully offer a sum of Fr. 10,000 in bonds of American or European State Loans, for the purpose of endowing a Lectureship to be called the President Wilson Lectureship, and submit that the President of the League of Nations shall select a Lecturer annually, fix his remuneration and determine the time and place for the delivery of the Lecture in any country that may be chosen for the purpose, the duty of the annual Lecturer being to discourse on the best means of acquiring and safeguarding national independence consistent with freedom, justice and the right of asylum accorded to political refugees.[620]"

The League of Nations turned down his offer. From then onwards, Shyamji, now ageing rapidly, cooled off in his political activity despite resurrecting his *Indian Sociologist* after the War.

Various events, including the passing of the draconian Rowlatt Act of 1919 and the consequent horrendous massacre of people at the Jallianwala Bagh in Amritsar in April 1919, led Mahatma Gandhi to abandon his long-held belief that the British rule was based on moral principles and good intentions, and that India would benefit from them ultimately. In 1920, Gandhi initiated his non-violent non-cooperation movement, a sharp contrast to what Shyamji and others had been advocating during the first two decades of the twentieth century.

Shyamji, who watched the way things were going in India, made a surprising move. He announced his support of Gandhi's non-cooperation movement and offered a 10,000 Rupee lectureship to be called the 'Tilak Memorial fellowship'. For the first three years, Shyamji proposed that Gandhi should be its trustee, select the beneficiaries, and the time and place for the lectures. After that period, the trust was to be administered by the President of the Indian National Congress[621]. By 1920, Shyamji, who had always been a keen advocate of using boycott as a tool of protest, had become disillusioned with violent methods of rebellion that he had advocated in the past[622]. That Shyamji should have donated money to Gandhi's movement, which contrasted dramatically with much that he had advocated earlier, is a sign that his heart and mind were truly focussed on gaining independence for India by whichever method that might prove effective.

With Tilak's death in 1920 and that of HM Hyndman in 1922, Shyamji, by now in his sixties, retired from politics, producing the final issue of *Indian Sociologist* in September 1922[623]. Ageing did not bring an end to his daily visits to Geneva's Stock Exchange, where he continued investing profitably until his final days on earth[624]. In 1926, Jawaharlal Nehru visited him in Geneva. He found Shyamji was living in melancholic circumstances (even though he was not short of money), but the old man, who reminisced much about his time at India House and continued to worry about being watched by the British, had:
"*...still some of the old fire in his eyes ...*[625]"

Four years after Nehru's brief visit, Shyamji began suffering from severe intestinal problems, which, despite surgical intervention in Geneva, led to his death on the 31st of March 1930[626]. While Shyamji was breathing his last, Gandhi in India was leading his followers on the famous Salt March to Dandi. Shyamji's wife Bhanumati died three years later. Shyamji and his wife were both cremated at the cemetery of St George (in Geneva), where their ashes were preserved.

Apart from leaving an immense fortune and a valuable library, which his widow distributed to various worthy causes (hospitals, universities, etc) in Switzerland and France, Shyamji had inserted a clause in his will regarding his (and later his wife's) ashes. He paid the cemetery in Geneva to preserve their ashes and to keep them for a hundred years and only to return them to India when it had shaken off British rule[627].

Shyamji's death was hardly noted either in India or in Britain. However, the now famous Indian socialist revolutionary Bhagat Singh (1907-1931), who was in prison in Lahore awaiting trial for murder of a British police officer, on hearing of Shyamji's demise, caused demonstrations to be held in open court[628].

According to one of his biographers, Shyamji should be remembered:

"... for his two outstanding achievements, first, the India House which bred and nourished some heroes and martyrs of the period ... Second, his fearless and ingenious propaganda for India's freedom ...[629]
"

I believe that he should also be remembered for his great contributions to the study of Sanskrit, one of the oldest documented of the members of the Indo-European language family, and for helping to found Oxford University's Indian Institute.

Although the end of his life was in saddened circumstances, the beginning of his life and most of his career was exceptionally brilliant. There can be few scholars like Shyamji, who have stepped out of their 'ivory towers' to inspire others to fight for the freedom of their native land.

RESURRECTION

Number 65 Cromwell Avenue, which was briefly known as 'India House', still stands today. Some decades ago, what was once a single residence was divided into three large flats, although this is impossible to detect by looking at its exterior. A plaque celebrating the fact that Veer Savarkar lived there is attached to one of the walls facing Cromwell Avenue. Recently, the owners of the ground floor flat kindly permitted me to look around it. They told me that many Indian visitors ring their front door to step inside the building where Veer Savarkar once lived. What the visitor sees is not what the Indian residents of the former India House would have known because many of the interior walls have been shifted and much has been modernised over the years. Yet, the views from the windows of 65 Cromwell Avenue might still be recognisable to those who visited or lived in India House in Edwardian times. In conservation conscious London, the external appearances of old buildings are preserved despite changes made within them.

The long garden attached to 65 Cromwell Avenue today slopes downwards very steeply. I looked at it, wondering where the tennis court mentioned in descriptions of India House could have been placed. There was little or no evidence of terracing. When I looked at detailed pre-WW2 maps of Highgate, I discovered that in Shyamji's time, the garden was much longer than it is now. The lower end of the original plot is now occupied by modern (post-WW2) house. However, the land it stands on, the lower part of the garden that Shyamji had bought, is flat enough for a tennis court.

There is a blue commemorative plaque attached to an outer wall of 65 Cromwell Avenue. Placed by the Greater London Council, it bears the words:

"Vinayak Damodar Savarkar, 1883 - 1966, Indian patriot and philosopher, lived here."

It was unveiled on the 8th of June 1985 by the then elderly Lord Fenner Brockway (1888-1988), a member of the Labour Party. He was born in Calcutta five years after Savarkar's birth and had been interested in Indian affairs for a long time[630]. When the group, which included 70 to 80 British MPs and the Indian cricketer Sunil Gavaskar, assembled outside the former India House, it was suggested that Fenner Brockway should be seated, but he insisted on remaining standing despite his great age. He said:

"I am proud to unveil this plaque but this should have done been by your Prime Minister Rajiv Gandhi.[631]*"*

He also said that all the charges levelled against Veer by the British Empire were groundless and to have a great patriot like him was a matter of great pride for any nation[632].

Not far from Cromwell Avenue, the house where Shyamji Krishnavarma lived in the former Queenswood Avenue (now Muswell Hill Road) still stands. A plaque records that Shyamji Krishnavarma, "Sanskrit Scholar and Indian Patriot", lived there from 1900 to '07. The white circular plaque is surrounded by the words (in Latin script): *"Hindu swatantryavir smruti sansthanam. Vande mataram*[633]*"*. Unlike Savarkar's plaque, this was not placed by the Greater London Council or any other official municipal body.

Shyamji was admitted to the Bar. However, his revolutionary activities, especially a letter he wrote to the London *Times* in February 1909, got him disbarred by the Inner Temple. He was in good company. Mahatma Gandhi was disbarred by the same Inn of Law in November 1922[634], and was re-instated posthumously in 1988[635]. In 2015, an Indian barrister in Delhi wrote to the Inner Temple pointing out that whilst Gandhi had been reinstated to the Bar many years earlier, Shyamji remained in disgrace. He pointed out that while Gandhi had been disbarred for having had a criminal record, Shyamji had merely written letters without breaking the law. Because of this letter, the Benchers of Inner Temple reinstated Shyamji in November 2015:

"...in recognition of the fact that the cause of Indian home rule, for which he fought, was not incompatible with membership of the bar and that by modern standards he did not receive an entirely fair hearing[636]*"*

In August 2003, the then Chief Minister of Gujarat, Narendra Modi, travelled to Switzerland. This was shortly after a major earthquake had devastated the region. He went to Geneva to fulfil Shyamji's last wishes, to bring his and his wife's ashes back to an India free of British rule[637]. He received the funerary urns in Geneva on the 22nd of August[638]. On arrival in India, the ashes were taken on a ceremonial tour, the 'Viranjali Yatra[639]', which commenced in Bombay and travelled 2029 kilometres through the State of Gujarat between the 25th of August and the 5th of September. During this trip the ashes were displayed to many people. Well-attended public meetings were held in 61 localities in 17 districts of Gujarat[640]. It is worth noting that it was only many years after India's independence in 1947 that the Krishnavarmas' ashes were brought to India. Is it possible that Shyamji had been forgotten or had fallen out of favour by the many predominantly Congress (and coalition) governments that ruled India before the Bharatiya Janata Party ('BJP') began its ascendancy?

Many years before Shyamji's remains were brought to India, those of another former resident of India House were brought home. In January 1977, the body of Curzon Wyllie's assassin Madan Lal Dhingra, whose body had been discovered accidentally during excavations at Pentonville Prison in December 1976[641], arrived at Palam Airport at New Delhi. Amongst those who paid homage to his remains was Prime Minister Indira Gandhi. After lying in state for several days at Kapurthala House (the Punjab State guesthouse), they were transported ceremoniously to the Punjab[642]. Arrangements for the inter-continental transfer of the remains took two years[643].

On the 4th of October 2009[644], Narendra Modi, still the Chief Minister of Gujarat, laid the foundation stone of a memorial complex dedicated to the memory of Shyamji and other freedom fighters near to Mandvi (in Kutch), where Krishnavarma was born. The complex, called Kranti Teerth[645], was completed and opened to the public on 13th December 2010[646], a century after India House in Highgate closed.

My wife and I, who were staying near Mandvi, were taken by our host's driver to see Kranti Teerth in February 2018. We had never heard of it and had no idea to what we were being taken. What met our eyes was one of the most surprising things I have seen in 25 years of visiting

India regularly. Four kilometres east of Mandvi, we drove to what reminded me of a surrealist painting in the style of the Belgian artist Rene Magritte. There, standing in the flat desert landscape, we saw a full-size three-storey red brick Victorian-style house with white stone trimmings such as can be found all over London's inner suburbs. Unblemished by age, it stood under a cloudless blue sky, dominating the horizon of the flat coastal plain. This building is a full-size replica of the former India House founded by Shyamji back in 1905.

Replica of India House at Kranti Teerth

Although the house at Kranti Teerth appears to be a replica of the original India House, it is only the exterior which is a true to life copy of that in Cromwell Avenue in Highgate. The exterior is brick cladding covering a concrete framed building whose interior is quite different from that of the original India House. The Mandvi 'replica' of the house in Highgate was designed by the Ahmedabad-based architect Hiren Gandhi[647].

The interior of this astonishing building contains a gallery of portraits of various Indian freedom fighters. The replica of India House has an auditorium in the basement, where we had watched a film about Shyamji and the independence of India. When I visited 65 Cromwell Avenue recently, I asked the current owners of the ground floor flat whether there is, or ever was, a basement there. They told me that they were sure that there had never been one because when the floors had been lifted to make internal modifications, there was no evidence of there ever having been any disturbance of the ground beneath the building.

In addition to the replica of India House, there is an airy, single-storey modern gallery dedicated to commemorating some of the early activists in the struggle for Indian independence. The gallery serves both as a museum and a mausoleum, because in the middle of it stands the urn that contains Shyamji's ashes. Statues depicting Shyamji and his wife as well as Madame Cama stand near the resurrected India House.

Ashes of Shyamji Krishnavarma at Kranti Teerth

Seeing the replica of India House in the middle of a desert landscape astonished me so much that it inspired me find out more about its story and to write this book.

Personal postscript

Between 1965 and 1970, I was a pupil at Highgate School (founded 1565), whose main Victorian gothic buildings stand at the top of Highgate Hill no more than two fifths of a mile northwest of 65 Cromwell Avenue. Since then, I have visited Highgate often. Like many others, I was completely unaware that it played a role in the history of India's independence. It took a visit to my wife's ancestral home, a small town in Kutch, 2500 miles southeast of my old school, for me to become aware of and interested in Highgate's part in this little-known episode in the story of India's past.

LIST OF SOME PEOPLE WHO VISITED OR LIVED IN INDIA HOUSE

An asterisk (*) denotes some uncertainty about whether the person ever entered India House.
Where possible, I have added very brief biographical notes.

Abbas, Mirza Sent to Paris from India House. Carried weapons to India.

Acharya, MPT 1887-1954. Founder member of Communist Party of India.

Aiyar, VVS 1881-1925. Indian revolutionary from Tamil Nadu. Died while rescuing his drowning daughter.

Ali, Asaf 1888-1953 follower of Savarkar, who later followed MK Gandhi. India's first ambassador to the USA. He also helped defend the officers of the Indian National Army in the treason trial of 1945.

Ali, Rauf brother of Asaf Ali.

Ali, Raza brother of Asaf Ali.

Amin, Chatturbhuj Cook at India House, who smuggled arms into India.

Amin, Govind Brother of Chatturbhuj. Moved from London to Paris. Committed suicide at Enghien in Belgium.

Balmokand, CS

Banker, Khemchand

Bapat, PM (aka Pandurang Mahadev) 1880-1967. A follower of Savarkar, who later became a follower of Gandhi.

Bhai Parmanand 1876-1947. Indian Nationalist and member of Arya Samaj, mainly active in South Africa, the Caribbean, and North America

Bhabha, SD Reverend. President of the Indian Christian Union (founded in the UK in 1895)

Bhattacharya, Basundev Assaulted Lee Warner.

Bhisey, SA 1867-1935. Scientist, inventor, and collaborator with Sir Ratan Tata.

Bhownagaree, M 1851-1933. British Conservative politician of Parsi origin.

Bipin Chandra Pal 1858-1932. Indian nationalist and writer opposed to Krishnavarma and the non-cooperation movement

Cama, Bhikaiji 1861-1936. Prominent and active Indian Nationalist of Parsi origin.

Chakravati, CK Indian nationalist active in the USA

Chattopadhyaya, V 1880-c. 1937. Indian nationalist. Went to Germany during WW1 and then the USSR in 1920. Murdered during one of Stalin's purges. Brother of Sarojini Naidu.

Darabseth, Beramjee Possibly Naoroji Beramji Darabseth, MD, LRCP (London)

Desai (Dr) Student at London University.

Desai (Mr) Barrister from Ahmedabad.

Despard, C 1844-1939. Irish Suffragist and Sinn Féin activist.

Dhan Devi

Dhingra, Bhajan Lal Born 1885. Brother of Madan Lal Dhingra. Studied law at Lincolns Inn.

Dhingra, Madan Lal 1883-1909. Indian nationalist. Studied engineering at UCL, then shot Sir Curzon Wyllie and Dr Lalcaca.

Doctor, Manilal Maganlal 1881-1956. Barrister. Spent some time in Aden, Fiji, and Mauritius.

Dube, Pandit Bhagwadin Arrived in London in 1907

Dutt, Sukhsagar brother of Ullaskar Dutt, the Bengali revolutionary and bomb-maker.

Dwarkadas, N Brother-in-law of Shyamji Krishnavarma. Law student. Died in Paris.

Gandhi, MK 1869-1948. The 'Mahatma'. Assassinated 1948.

Garnett, D 1892-1981. Writer, journalist, and member of the Bloomsbury Group.

Gaurishankar, Mr & Mrs

Godrej, Manchersham Barjorji Indian nationalist. Brother of industrialist AB Godrej.

Hansraj, Lala 1864-1938. Barrister and member of Arya Samaj.

Har Dayal 1884-1939. Indian nationalist, freedom fighter, and writer.

Harnam Singh Became a barrister.

Hayat, Sikander Sir Sikander Hayat Khan. 1892-1942. Prime Minister of the Punjab 1937-42.

Hemchandra Das 1871-1951. Indian nationalist.

Hyndman, HM 1842-1921. Socialist.

Jayaswal, KP 1881-1937. Historian and lawyer.

Jayaswal, R

Khan, Malik Umar Hayat (*)

Khaparde, GS 1854-1938. Lawyer, who defended BN Tilak and devotee of Sai Baba of Shirdi.

Kirtikar Police informer, then double agent.

Koregoankar, HK born c. 1882. Student in London. After talking to police in Bombay in 1909, he moved to Gwalior.

Krishnavarma, Bhanumati Wife of Shyamji Krishnavarma.

Krishnavarma, Shyamji 1857-1930. Sanskrit scholar, Indian nationalist, and founder of India House

Kunte (from Gwalior?). Helped translate into English Savarkar's book on the Indian War of Independence (1857).

Lala Lajpat Rai 1865-1928. Indian nationalist. Died after a police baton attack in India.

Lenin, VI (*) 1870-1924. Russian revolutionary politician and leader.

Master, JS Parsi member of Abhinav Bharat. He examined Madan Lal Dhingra's body at Pentonville Prison.

Master, Maneksha Sorabjee Born 1860 Represented the *Parsee* magazine in London.

Mohammad, Dost Barrister

Mukherjee, JC Once a journalist for Gandhi's Indian Opinion. Later a follower of Veer Savarkar.

Naoroji, Dadabhai 1825-1917. First Indian to be a British Member of Parliament.

Niranjan Pal 1889-1959. Son of Bipin Chandra Pal. Became a founding member of Bombay Talkies.

Oza, SD (Dr)

Patel, Manilal

Patel, VG

Parekh, Jethalal Motilal Lawyer. Member of Middle Temple.

Pereira, DE (Dr) Medical with qualification LRCP&S (London)

Parker, PL Member of Parliament

Phadke, WV Born about 1886. Translator of Savarkar's book on the Indian War of Independence (1857). Called to the Bar in 1910.

Polak, M Father of Gandhi's colleague in S. Africa, Henry Polak.

Quelch, H 1858-1913. Socialist, journalist, and trade unionist.

Rafiq, Muhammad Khan of Nabha Barrister in 1910 (Lincolns Inn).

Raiza, H

Raja, Hans

Rajan, TSS (Dr) Became a member of Madras Legislative Assembly in 1937

Rana, SR 1870-1957. Barrister, jeweller, and Indian Nationalist. Lived many years in France and retired to India in 1955.

Rao, Rama After confessing about Savarkar to police in India, he joined the Indian Police Department.

Ritch, LW South African Jewish man, who introduced MK Gandhi to theosophy. Became a lawyer.

Saklatawala, SD 1874-1936. Indian politician in the UK. Became member of Communist Party of Great Britain.

Savarkar, VD 1883-1966. Indian nationalist, writer.

Shukla, R 1877-1956. Became Chief Minister of the Central Provinces in 1947.

Students from S. Africa A few who came with Ghandi, MK

Suhrawardi, A (*) Became Chief Minister of Bengal

Swami, KVR Attended India House irregularly because of poor health.

Swinney, SH 1857-1923. Irish Positivist philosopher and anti-imperialist.

Tirumalachari, MP (see: Acharya, MPT)
Varma, G
Varma, Hotilal Journalist. Imprisoned in the Andaman Islands.
Zaveri, N

ACKNOWLEDGEMENTS

H Bhabha, Anurupa Cinar, Brian Champness, C Pilkington, Devalina Sen, Dr PM Urbach, Ministry of Justice (UK), Mr and Mrs Mark Stieler, Mr and Mrs S Suraiyar, Ole Birk Laursen, R Maluste, Staff at the British Library (London).

And, last but not least, my dear wife Lopa, some of whose ancestors originated in Krishnavarma's birthplace. She has patiently lived through this book's long gestation period and made many helpful comments and suggestions.

I gratefully acknowledge the help and advice that these kind people have given me, but I do not hold them in the slightest bit responsible for any errors or inaccuracies that might have crept into my text.

SOME BOOKS CONSULTED

Actes Du Sixieme Congres International Des Orientalistes, publ. by EJ Brill, Leiden: 1885
Ahmed, F: *Bengal Politics in Britain*, publ. by Lulu.com: 2011

Ananthamurthy, UR: *Hindutva or Hind Swaraj*, publ. by Harper Perennial, Noida: 2016

Andersen, WK & Damle, SD: *The RSS A View to the Inside*, publ. by Penguin, Gurgaon: 2018

Anon: *Sri Aurobindo and Baroda*, publ. by Sri Aurobindo Society, Baroda: 2014

Basu, S: *Victoria & Abdul*, publ. by Rupa, New Delhi: 2010

Bhandu, V: *The Life and times of Madan Lal Dhingra*, publ. by Ocean Books, New Delhi: 2013

Bose, AC (2): *Indian Revolutionaries Abroad, 1905-1922: In the Background of International Developments*, publ. by Bharati Bhawan, Patna: 1971

Bose, AC: *Indian Revolutionaries Abroad: 1905-1927*, publ. by Northern Book Centre, New Delhi: 2002, first publ. 1998

Chand, F: *Lajpat Rai. Life and Work*, publ. by Publications Division, Ministry of Education & Broadcasting: New Delhi: 2010

Chandra, B et al.: *India's Struggle for Independence*, publ. by Penguin, New Delhi: 1989

Cherry, B & Pevsner, N: *London 4: North*, publ. by Penguin Books, London: 1998

Chirol, V: *Indian Unrest*, publ. by Macmillan, London:1910

Congreve, R: *India*, first publ. 1857 and republished by Shyamaji Krishnavarma, London:1907

Dalrymple, W: *The Last Mughal: The Fall of Delhi, 1857*, publ. by Bloomsbury, Lodon:2009

DNB: *Oxford Dictionary of National Biography*, online edition
Dodd, G: *The History of the Indian Revolt and of the Expeditions to Persia, China and Japan 1856-7-8*, publ. by W&R Chambers, London: 1859

Echenberg, M: *Plague Ports: The global urban impact of bubonic plague 1894-1901*, publ. by NYU Press, New York: 2007

Elst, K: *Why I Killed the Mahatma*, publ. by Rupa, New Delhi: 2018

Fenner Brockway, A: *The Indian Crisis*, publ. by Victor Gollancz, London: 1930

Fischer-Tiné, H: *Shyamji Krishnavarma: Sanskrit, Sociology and Anti-Imperialism*, publ. by Routledge, New Delhi: 2014

Gandhi, MK (ed. Parel, AJ): *Hind Swaraj and other writings*, publ. by Cambridge University Press: Cambridge: 2009

Gandhi, R: *Gandhi: The Man, His People, and the Empire*, publ. by University of California Press: 2008

Garnett, D: *The Golden Echo*, publ. by Harcourt, Brace and Company, New York: 1954

Gilbert, M: *Servant of India*, publ. by Longmans, London: 1966

Gilmour, D: *Curzon*, publ. by John Murray, London: 1994

Gokhale, DN: *Biography of Barbarao Savarkar*, published by www.savarkar.org: 2008

Gordon, S: *The Marathas 1600-1818*, publ. by CUP and Foundation Books, New Delhi:1998

Herman, A: *Gandhi and Churchill*, publ. by Random House, New York: 2008

Hunt, JD: *Gandhi in London*, publ. by Promilla & Co, New Delhi: 2012

Hyndman, HM: *The Bankruptcy of India*, publ. by Swann Sonnenschein & Lowrey, London: 1886

Hyndman, HM: *The emancipation of India*, publ. by The Twentieth Century Press, London: 1911

Jaffrelot, C: *The Hindu Nationalist Movement and Indian Politics 1925 to the 1990s*, publ. by Hurst, London: 1996

Joglekar, JD: *Veer Savarkar Father of Hindu Nationalism*, publ. by Lulu.com: 2006

Joshi, VC (ed.): *Lajpat Rai Autobiographical Writings*, publ. by University Publishers, Delhi and Jullundur: 1965

Johnson, WJ: *Oxford Dictionary of Hinduism*, publ. by OUP, Oxford: 2009

Jones, KW: *Socio-Religious Reform Movements in British India*, publ. by CUP, Cambridge: 1989

Keer, D: *Veer Savarkar*, publ. by Popular Prakashan, Bombay: 1988

Ker, JC: *Political Trouble in India 1907-1917*, first publ. 1917, reprinted by Oriental Publishers, Delhi: 1973

Knight, P: *The British Army in Mesopotamia, 1914-1918*, publ. by McFarland, Jefferson (NC): 1970

Krishnavarma, and The Indian Sociologist in *Colonial Exchanges: Political Theory and the Agency of the Colonized*, publ. by OUP: 2017

Kuruvachira, J: *Hindu Nationalists of Modern India*, publ. by Rawat, New Delhi: 2006

Lahiri, S: *Indians in Britain*, publ. by Frank Cass, London: 2000

Mack Smith, D: *Mazzini*, publ. by Yale University Press, New Haven: 1994

Majumdar RC (ed.): *Struggle for Freedom*, publ. by Bharatiya Vidya Bhavan, Bombay: 1988

Mansingh, S: *Historical Dictionary of India*, publ. by Vision Books, New Delhi: 1998

Marino, A: *Narendra Modi. A political biography*, publ. by Harper Collins, Noida: 2014

Marwar, IS: *Rethinking resistance: Spencer, Krishnavarma, and The Indian Sociologist* in *Colonial Exchanges: Political Theory and the Agency of the Colonized*, publ. by OUP: 2017

Matikkala, M: *Empire and Imperial Ambition: Liberty, Englishness and Anti-imperialism in Late Victorian Britain*, publ. by IB Tauris, London: 2010

Mazzini, J: *The Duties of Man*, publ. by Chapman & Hall, London: 1862

McLane, JR: *Indian Nationalism and the Early Congress*, publ. by Princeton University Press, Princeton: 1977

Minault, G: *The Khilafat Movement*, published by OUP, New Delhi: 1999

Motiwala, BN: *Karsondas Mulji: A Biographical Study*, publ. by Parbhudas Ladabhai Mody, Bombay: 1935

Nehru, J: *An Autobiography* (first publ. 1936), reprint publ. by OUP, New Delhi: 1982

Nicholson, V: *Among the Bohemians*, publ. by Viking, London: 2002

Noorani, AG: *Savarkar and Hindutva*, publ. by Left Word, New Delhi: 2002

Padhya, HG: *Photographic Reminiscence of Pandit Shyamaji Krishnavarma*, published by Pothi.com: 2010

Padmanabhan, RA: *VVS Aiyar*, publ. by National Book Trust India, New Delhi: 1980

Raval, RL: *Mahipatram*, publ. by Sahitya Akademi: 2002

Rees, JD: *India; the Real India*, publ. by JB Millett Company, Boston: 1910

Roberts (Lord): *Forty-One Years in India: from Subaltern to Commander-in-chief*, publ. by Macmillan, New York: 1901

Rushbrook Williams, LF: *The Black Hills*, publ. by Weidenfeld & Nicolson, London: 1958

Sammadar R: *Refugees and the State*, publ. by Sage, New Delhi: 2003

Sareen, TR: *Indian Revolutionary Movement Abroad (1905-21)* by, publ. by Sterling, New Delhi (1979)

Savarkar, VD: *The story of my Transportation for Life*, publ. first in Marathi in 1927, then translated by VN Naik, downloaded from savarkar.org

Savarkar, VD (L): *Inside the Enemy Camp*, transl. by VS Godbole, available http://savarkar.org/en/pdfs/inside_the_enemy_camp.v001.pdf

Savarkar, VD: *Six Glorious Epochs of Indian History*, transl. by ST Godbole, publ. by Bal Savarkar, Bombay: 1971

Savarkar, VD: *Essentials of Hindutva*, downloaded from Savarkar.org
Sen, SN: *History Modern India*, publ. by New Age Internationa[648]l, New Delhi: 2006

Sethna, KA: *Madame Bhikaiji Rustom Cama*, publ. by Ministry of Information and Broadcasting, New Delhi: 2013

Shaik, GA *The Mahabat Album*, publ. by GA Shaik, Junagadh: 1936

Sharma, HD: *100 Great Lives*, publ. by Rupa, New Delhi: 2006

Sharma, J: *Hindutva*, publ. by Viking, New Delhi: 2003

Sharma, SD: *India Marching: Reflections from a Nationalistic Perspective*, publ. by iUniverse, Bloomington: 2012

Sherwood, M: *Origins of Pan-Africanism: Henry Sylvester Williams, Africa, and the African Diaspora*, publ. by Routledge, New York: 2011

Singh, R: *Portraits of Hindutva from Harappa to Ayodhya*, publ. by Rupa, New Delhi: 2018

Sinha, R: *Dr. Keshav Baliram Hedgewar*, publ. by Publications Division Ministry of Information and Broadcasting Government of India, New Delhi: 2015

Solomon, RV & Bond, JW: *Indian States: A Biographical, Historical, and Administrative Survey*, publ. by Asian Educational Services, New Delhi: 2006

Spencer, H: *Facts and Comments*, publ. by D Appleon, New York: 1902

Sri Aurobindo: *Tales of Prison Life*, publ. by Sri Aurobindo Ashram Publication Department, Pondicherry: 1974

Srikrishan 'Sarala': *Indian Revolutionaries 1757-1961 (Vol-1)*, publ. by Ocean Books, New Delhi:1999

Srivastava, H: *Five Stormy Years*, publ. by Allied Publishers: 1953

Tejani, S: *Indian Secularism: A Social and Intellectual History, 1890-1950*, publ. by Indiana Univ. Press: 2008

Tickell, A: *Terrorism, Insurgency and Indian-English Literature, 1830-1947*, publ. by Routledge, New York: 2013

Varma, GL: *Shyamji Krishna Varma The Unknown Patriot*, publ. by Ministry of Information and Broadcasting Government of India, New Delhi: 1993

Verhandlungen des fünften internationalen Orientalisten-Congresses, publ. by A Ascher, Berlin:1881

Visram, R: *Asians in Britain* by R Visram , published by Pluto Press, London: 2002

Wolpert, SA: *Tilak and Gokhale*, publ. by OUP, Oxford: 1961

Yajnik, I: *Shyamaji Krishnavarma*, publ. by Lakshmi Publications, Bombay: 1950

Statues of Mr and Mrs Krishnavarma at Kranti Teerth

A list of the textual references begins after this.

REFERENCES

Websites were accessed on dates listed below

[1] https://www.britannica.com/event/Mysore-Wars, accessed 11 June 2019

[2] https://www.britannica.com/event/Vellore-Mutiny, accessed 6 June 2019

[3] https://www.britannica.com/topic/Sikh-Wars, accessed 2 July 2019

[4] Quotes from Sareen, TR: *Indian Revolutionary Movement Abroad (1905-21)* by, publ. by Sterling, New Delhi (1979)

[5] Part of a submission to the Welby Commission, 31st January 1897

[6] https://en.wikipedia.org/wiki/Scientific_racism, accessed 2 July 2019

[7] By 'Hindoo', Marx was referring to an inhabitant of Hindustan, rather than an adherent of Hinduism.

[8] https://www.marxists.org/archive/marx/works/1853/06/25.htm, accessed 18 May 2019

[9] Roberts: *Forty-One Years in India: from Subaltern to Commander-in-chief*, publ. by Macmillan, New York:1901

[10] Quoted by Richard Congreve in India, publ. 1857

[11] https://www.marxists.org/archive/marx/works/1857/09/17.htm, accessed 18 May 2019

[12] Brigadier-General J G S Neill (1810 –1857)

[13] Dalrymple, W: *The Last Mughal: The Fall of Delhi, 1857*, publ. by Bloomsbury, Lodon:2009

[14] https://www.marxists.org/archive/marx/works/1858/10/01.htm, accessed 18 May 2019

[15] Recall that slavery had already been abolished by law throughout the British Empire

[16] Quotes from Dodd, G: *The History of the Indian Revolt and of the Expeditions to Persia, China and Japan 1856-7-8*, publ. by W&R Chambers, London: 1859

[17] Quotes from Congreve, R: *India*, first publ. 1857 and republished by Shyamaji Krishnavarma, London:1907

[18] https://www.britannica.com/place/India/Government-of-India-Act-of-1858, accessed 16 Mar 2019. See also: *Evolution and basic principles of Indian constitution* by N G Ningade: http://shodhganga.inflibnet.ac.in/bitstream/10603/174777/8/08_chapter%202.pdf, accessed 16 Mar 2019

[19] https://www.bl.uk/collection-items/proclamation-by-the-queen-in-council-to-the-princes-chiefs-and-people-of-india, accessed 18 May 2019

[20] See, for example: S Basu *Victoria & Abdul*, publ. by Rupa, New Delhi: 2010

[21] Savarkar, VD: *Six Glorious Epochs of Indian History*, transl. by ST Godbole, publ. by Bal Savarkar, Bombay: 1971

[22] https://api.parliament.uk/historic-hansard/commons/1898/feb/15/address-in-answer-to-her-majestys-most#S4V0053P0_18980215_HOC_111, accessed 18 May 2019

[23] Speech delivered at the annual dinner of the London Indian Society 22nd March 1902.

[24] *Indian Opinion* (1 October 1903)

[25] Visram, R: *Asians in Britain* by R Visram , published by Pluto Press, London: 2002

[26] McLane, JR: *Indian Nationalism and the Early Congress*, publ. by Princeton University Press, Princeton: 1977

[27] Sareen,TJ

[28] For a readable, informative biography, see: GL Varma: *Shyamji Krishna Varma The Unknown Patriot*, publ. by Ministry of information and Broadcasting Government of India, New Delhi: 1993

[29] Rushbrook Williams, LF: *The Black Hills*, publ. by Weidenfeld & Nicolson, London:

1958

[30] See: http://www.bhanushalisamaj.in/ , accessed 22 March 2019

[31] See: www.indianchildnames.com , accessed 22 March 2019

[32] Bose, AC: *Indian Revolutionaries Abroad: 1905-1927*, publ. by Northern Book Centre, New Delhi: 2002, first publ. 1998

[33] See: https://en.wikipedia.org/wiki/Bhanushali, accessed 23 March 2019

[34] Fischer-Tiné, H: *Shyamji Krishnavarma: Sanskrit, Sociology and Anti-Imperialism*, publ. by Routledge, New Delhi: 2014

[35] See: https://www.krantiteerth.org/about-shyamji-krishna-verma.html, accessed 22 March 2019

[36] Yajnik, I: *Shyamaji Krishnavarma*, publ. by Lakshmi Publications, Bombay: 1950

[37] See: Barton Scott, J: Journal of the American Academy of Religion, March 2015, Vol. 83, No. 1, pp. 181–209, and Motiwala, BN: *Karsondas Mulji: A Biographical Study*, publ. by Parbhudas Ladabhai Mody, Bombay: 1935

[38] Yajnik, I

[39] Raval, RL: *Mahipatram*, publ. by Sahitya Akademi: 2002

[40] See: https://bombayhighcourt.nic.in/libweb/historicalcases/cases/Maharaj_Libel_Cases_-_1862.html, accessed 23 March 2019

[41] *Paathshala*: a Hindu school where pupils are taught Sanskrit, usually by Brahmins

[42] Yajnik, I

[43] Johnson, WJ: *Oxford Dictionary of Hinduism*, publ. by OUP, Oxford: 2009

[44] He was Gujarati. See Fischer-Tiné; Yajnik, I adds the 'Parekh' to his name

[45] Pandit: 'learned' or 'wise'. See: Johnson, WJ

[46] Yajnik, I

[47] For a succinct biography of Dayanand, see Johnson, WJ

[48] See: http://www.indianpost.com/viewstamp.php/SWAMI%20VIRJANAND%20%28%20SAINT%20%29

[49] Kuruvachira, J: *Hindu Nationalists of Modern India*, publ. by Rawat, New Delhi: 2006

[50] Fischer-Tiné, H

[51] Translation of text available at: http://www.aryasamaj.org/newsite/Light_Of_Truth.pdf, accessed 23 March 2019. All of Dayand's quotes are from this source.

[52] Kuruvachira, J

[53] Sharma, J: *Hindutva*, publ. by Viking, New Delhi: 2003

[54] Homa: making oblation to the Gods. See: Johnson, WJ

[55] Sharma, J

[56] Sharma, J

[57] Sharma, J

[58] Johnson, WJ

[59] https://www.gktoday.in/gk/difference-between-brahmo-samaj-and-arya-samaj/, accessed 30 June 2019

[60] Varma, GL

[61] Yajnik, I

[62] Fischer-Tiné, H

[63] DNB: *Oxford Dictionary of National Biography*, online edition, accessed 24 March 2019

[64] http://www.oxfordhistory.org.uk/broad/buildings/east/old_indian_institute/index.html

[65] See: Bose, AC

[66] Many Indian freedom fighters and reformers of note belonged to the Chitpavan community.

[67] Quoted by Varma, GL

[68] Quoted by Varma, GL

[69] Yajnik, I

[70] Yajnik, I

[71] McLane, JR

[72] Here, 'shastri' refers to the Brahmin priests, against whom members of the Arya Samaj were in conflict

[73] Quoted in Yajnik, I

[74] Bose, AC

[75] Yajnik, I

[76] José Gersen de Cunha (1844-1900) was a medical doctor and a renowned Indologist. See: https://www.bmj.com/content/2/2072/781.2, accessed 28 March 2019

[77] Fischer-Tiné, H

[78] Varma, GL

[79] DNB

[80] Yajnik, I

[81] *Verhandlungen des fünften internationalen Orientalisten-Congresses*, publ. by A Ascher, Berlin:1881

[82] *Proceedings Of The Twenty Sixth International Congress Of Orientalists Volume I*, publ. by XXVI International Congress of Orientalists, New Delhi: 1966

[83] *Actes Du Sixieme Congres International Des Orientalistes*, publ. by EJ Brill, Leiden: 1885

[84] Varma, GL

[85] Quoted by Yajnik I

[86] *Times* (of London), November 18, 1884

[87] https://www.innertemplelibrary.org.uk/archived-files/indianindependence.pdf accessed 2 July 2019

[88] https://oll.libertyfund.org/pages/lm-spencer, accessed 31 0march

[89] https://mises.org/library/herbert-spencer-freedom-and-empire, accessed 24 March 2019

[90] https://www.newyorker.com/magazine/2007/08/13/man-with-a-plan , accessed 31 March 2019

[91] Spencer, H: *Facts and Comments*, publ. by D Appleon, New York: 1902

[92] *Indian Sociologist*, 1909, quoted by Marwar, IS: *Rethinking resistance: Spencer, Krishnavarma, and The Indian Sociologist* in *Colonial Exchanges: Political Theory and the Agency of the Colonized*, publ. by OUP: 2017

[93] "*Positivism is a philosophical system deeply rooted in science and mathematics. It's based on the view that whatever exists can be verified through experiments, observation, and mathematical/logical proof. Everything else is non-existent.*" See: https://philosophyterms.com/positivism/, accessed 25 March 2019

[94] Varma, GL

[95] Matikkala, M: *Empire and Imperial Ambition: Liberty, Englishness and Anti-imperialism in Late Victorian Britain*, publ. by IB Tauris, London: 2010

[96] See: https://brill.com/abstract/book/edcoll/9789004335462/B9789004335462_024.xml#FN000879, accessed 25 March 2019

[97] http://heresiarch.org/hughswinny.php, accessed 25 March 2019

[98] Quotes from Hyndman, HM: *The Bankruptcy of India*, publ. by Swann Sonnenschein & Lowrey, London: 1886

[99] Hyndman, HM: *The emancipation of India*, publ. by The Twentieth Century Press, London: 1911

[100] Yagnik, I

[101] Mrs Krishnavarma had been brought to England in 1883 or '84 when Shyamji had visited India briefly with Monier-Williams (Bose, AC)

[102] Varma, GL

[103] Yajnik, I

[104] Varma, GL

[105] Bose, AC

[106] Srikrishan 'Sarala': *Indian Revolutionaries 1757-1961 (Vol-1)*, publ. by Ocean Books, New Delhi:1999

[107] Varma, GL

[108] Fischer-Tiné, H

[109] https://plato.stanford.edu/entries/spencer/ , accessed 25 March 2019

[110] Bose, AC

[111] Varma, GL

[112] http://www.thearyasamaj.org/navlakhamahal_en & https://timesofindia.indiatimes.com/city/jaipur/Udaipur-Garden-Palace-now-a-shrine-to-Arya-Samaj-founder/articleshow/55282697.cms , both accessed 27 March 2019

[113] Varma, GL

[114] Yajnik, I

[115] Varma, GL

[116] Shaik, GA: *The Mahabat Album,* publ. by GA Shaik, Junagadh: 1936

[117] Yagnik, I

[118] See Varma, GL for more detail about Shyamji's experiences in Junagadh.

[119] Sareen, TR

[120] Yagnik, I

[121] Fischer-Tiné

[122] DNB

[123] Quoted in Yagnik, I

[124] Yagnik, I

[125] Yagnik, I

[126] Yagnik, I

[127] Yagnik, I

[128] Yagnik, I

[129] See: Wolpert, SA: *Tilak and Gokhale,* publ. by OUP, Oxford: 1961 and Elst, K: *Why I Killed the Mahatma,* publ. by Rupa, New Delhi: 2018

[130] Yagnik, I

[131] Echenberg, M: *Plague Ports: The global urban impact of bubonic plague 1894-1901,* publ. by NYU Press, New York: 2007

[132] http://legislative.gov.in/sites/default/files/A1897-03.pdf, accessed 27 March 2019

[133] Echenberg, M

[134] Fischer-Tiné, H

[135] *Times* of London 25 June 1897

[136] Echenberg, M

[137] Sen, SN: *History Modern India,* publ. by New Age International, New Delhi: 2006

[138] Chirol, V: *Indian Unrest,* publ. by Macmillan, London:1910

[139] http://dspace.wbpublibnet.gov.in:8080/jspui/bitstream/10689/12660/4/Chapter1_1-78p.pdf, accessed 27 March 2019

[140] Wolpert, SA

[141] http://indiansaga.com/whoswho/shyamji_krishnavarma_1.html, accessed 29 March 2019

[142] Yajnik, I

[143] Yajnik, I

4

[144] Bose, AC. There is no mention of this in Shyamji's detailed biography by I Yajnik

[145] https://www.londonremembers.com/memorials/pandit-shyamji-krishna-varma, accessed 29 Mar 2019

[146] Padhya, HG: *Photographic Reminiscence of Pandit Shyamaji Krishnavarma*, published by Pothi.com: 2010

[147] Fischer-Tiné, H

[148] Fischer-Tiné, H

[149] *Times* of London, 13 April 1899

[150] *Times* of London, 19th April 1899

[151] Varma, GL

[152] *Times* of London, 9 December 1903

[153] The play contains sentiments and a portrayal of the Prophet, which were thought to be offensive to Muslims

[154] *Times* (London) 15th December 1903

[155] Fischer-Tiné, H

[156] Harrison F: *The Herbert Spencer lecture, delivered at Oxford, March 9, 1905*, publ. by Clarendon Press, Oxford: 1905

[157] Sen, SN

[158] Gilmour, D: *Curzon*, publ. by John Murray, London: 1994

[159] Words by Bankim Chandra Chattopadhyay, set to music by Rabindranath Tagore (https://www.encyclopedia.com/international/encyclopedias-almanacs-transcripts-and-maps/bande-mataram , accessed 19 May 2019)

[160] https://en.wikisource.org/wiki/1911_Encyclop%C3%A6dia_Britannica/Russo-Japanese_War, accessed 31 March 2019

[161] Yajnik, I

[162] This and other quotes from the *Indian Sociologist* are from Yajnik, I

[163] *Indian Sociologist*, Vol 1, no. 1, January 1905

[164] Yajnik I

[165] Fischer-Tiné, H

[166] Yajnik, I

[167] Mukund R Jayakar qualified as a barrister in London in 1905 and subsequently led a far from revolutionary life (*The Hindu*, 11 March 1959)

[168] Manchercha Baorji Godrej, brother of the founders of the Godrej group of companies (see: Sammadar R: *Refugees and the State*, publ. by Sage, New Delhi: 2003)

[169] Srivastava, H: *Five Stormy Years*, publ. by Allied Publishers: 1953

[170] Quotes from Yajnik, I

[171] Yajnik, I

[172] Fischer-Tiné, H

[173] Varma, GL

[174] Bose, AC

[175] Yajnik, I

[176] Varma, GL

[177] Yajnik, I

[178] Varma, GL

[179] https://en.wikipedia.org/wiki/S._R._Rana, accessed 1 April 2019

[180] Varma, GL

[181] Bose, AC (2): *Indian Revolutionaries Abroad, 1905-1922: In the Background of International Developments*, publ. by Bharati Bhawan, Patna: 1971

[182] Bose, AC and Varma, GL

[183] Bose, AC (2)

[184] Fischer-Tiné, H

[185] *Indian Sociologist*, Vol 1, no. 1, January 1905

[186] Words of Valentine Chirol, Foreign Editor of the *Times* (London) quoted in Ryan D and Ross S (eds.) *The handbook to the Bloomsbury Group*, publ. by Bloomsbury Academic, London: 2018 See also: *Times* (London) 10 Aug 1910

[187] Yajnik, I, and Lahiri, S

[188] The tramway that passed the west end of Cromwell Avenue on its way between Archway Tavern and Southwood Avenue was a cable-assisted system like that still used in San Francisco. It ceased operating as a cableway in 1909, when it became electric-powered (https://www.hows.org.uk/personal/rail/incline/high.htm , accessed 3 April 2019). It exists no more.

[189] Waterlow Park

[190] Yajnik, I

[191] Cherry, B & Pevsner, N: *London 4: North*, publ. by Penguin Books, London: 1998

[192] Fischer-Tiné, H

[193] Quotes about India House from Yajnik, I

[194] Quoted in Lahiri, S

[195] http://www.london-weather.eu/article.45.html, accessed 1 April 2019, and *Times* of London 1 July 1905

[196] https://en.wikipedia.org/wiki/Bhikaiji_Cama, accessed 4 July 2019

[197] Yajnik, I

[198] Lahiri, S

[199] http://www.open.ac.uk/researchprojects/makingbritain/content/charlotte-despard, accessed 1 April 2019

[200] Yajnik, I

[201] Quotes from Hyndman's speech from Yajnik, I

[202] Yajnik, I

[203] Sharma, HD: *100 Great Lives*, publ. by Rupa, New Delhi: 2006

[204] Chandra, B et al.: *India's Struggle for Independence*, publ. by Penguin, New Delhi: 1989

[205] Varma, GL

[206] Yajnik, I

[207] Fischer-Tiné, H

[208] Ker, JC: *Political Trouble in India 1907-1917*, first publ. 1917, reprinted by Oriental Publishers, Delhi: 1973

[209] 'Veer' means 'brave' in Marathi, Savarkar's mother tongue

[210] Keer, D: *Veer Savarkar*, publ. by Popular Prakashan, Bombay: 1988

[211] Noorani, AG: *Savarkar and Hindutva*, publ. by Left Word, New Delhi: 2002

[212] http://savarkar.org/

[213] Tejani, S: *Indian Secularism: A Social and Intellectual History, 1890-1950*, publ. by Indiana Univ. Press: 2008

[214] Wolpert, SA

[215] https://api.parliament.uk/historic-hansard/commons/1893/aug/28/the-bombay-riots, accessed 5 April 2019

[216] Keer, D

[217] Keer, D

[218] Gokhale, DN: *Biography of Barbarao Savarkar*, published by www.savarkar.org: 2008, downloaded 5 April 2019

[219] Joglekar, JD: *Veer Savarkar Father of Hindu Nationalism*, publ. by Lulu.com: 2006

[220] Keer, D

[221] Gokhale, DN

[222] Joglekar, JD

[223] Joglekar, JD

[224] Keer, D

[225] Joglekar, JD

[226] Keer, D

[227] Joglekar, JD

[228] Joglekar, JD

[229] Joglekar, JD

[230] Keer, D

[231] Gokhale, DN

[232] Details of Savarkar's sea voyage and journey to London from Savarkar VD (1965)

[233] https://en.wikipedia.org/wiki/SS_Persia_(1900), accessed 3 April 2019

[234] Mack Smith, D: *Mazzini*, publ. by Yale University Press, New Haven: 1994

[235] Bose, AC

[236] Bose, AC

[237] Savarkar, VD (L) : *Inside the Enemy Camp*, transl. by VS Godbole, first published in Marathi in 1965, available http://savarkar.org/en/pdfs/inside_the_enemy_camp.v001.pdf, accessed frequently during 2019

[238] Wolpert, SA

[239] https://www.encyclopedia.com/history/encyclopedias-almanacs-transcripts-and-maps/lala-lajpat-rai, accessed 3 April 2019

[240] Joshi, VC (ed.): *Lajpat Rai Autobiographical Writings*, publ. by University Publishers, Delhi and Jullundur: 1965

[241] Yagnik, I

[242] Yagnik, I

[243] Bose, AC (2)

[244] Bose, AC

[245] Letter quoted in Yajnik, I

[246] For details of this meeting, see: Yajnik, I

[247] https://www.britannica.com/biography/Surendranath-Banerjea, accessed 4 July 2019

[248] http://www.columbia.edu/itc/mealac/pritchett/00routesdata/1800_1899/congress/presidents/presidents.html, accessed 4 July 2019

[249] Mansingh, S: *Historical Dictionary of India*, publ. by Vision Books, New Delhi: 1998

[250] Yajnik, I

[251] Srivastava, H

[252] Savarkar, VD (L

[253] Keer, D

[254] http://indiafacts.org/life-of-savarkar-from-nashik-to-andamans/, accessed 4 April 2019

[255] Savarkar, VD (L)

[256] Joglekar, JD

[257] SM Paranjape (1864-1929): https://en.wikipedia.org/wiki/Shivram_Mahadev_Paranjape, accessed 6 April 2019

[258] Eventually, some of the ideas incorporated in Veer's book would resurface in his formulation of Hindutva, published in 1923.

[259] Savarkar, VD (L)

[260] Jaffrelot, C: *The Hindu Nationalist Movement and Indian Politics 1925 to the 1990s*, publ. by Hurst, London: 1996

[261] Both extracts from Savarkar, VD (L)

[262] Savarkar, VD (L)

[263] Bose, AC

[264] Savarkar, VD (L)

[265] Savarkar, VD (L)

[266] Joglekar, JD

[267] Bose, AC

[268] Savarkar, VD (L)

[269] Savarkar VD(L)

[270] *Times* of London, Dec 23rd, 1909

[271] Admitted to Lincolns Inn 10th November 1902, see: https://hosted.law.wisc.edu/wordpress/sharafi/files/2010/07/Lincolns-Inn-6.0.pdf, accessed 4 April 2019

[272] Ahmed, F: *Bengal Politics in Britain*, publ. by Lulu.com: 2011

[273] Bose, AC (2)

[274] http://savarkar.org/en//Encyc/2017/5/22/Associates-in-Armed-Revolution.html, accessed 4 April 2019

[275] Keer, D

[276] Unless specified, for details of Gandhi's visit see: Hunt, JD: *Gandhi in London*, publ. by Promilla & Co, New Delhi: 2012

[277] http://www.kamat.com/database/biographies/t_s_s_rajan.htm, accessed 4 July 2019

[278] Padmanabhan, RA: *VVS Aiyar*, publ. by National Book Trust India, New Delhi: 1980

[279] Nicholson, V: *Among the Bohemians*, publ. by Viking, London: 2002

[280] Maybe, 'AA' was Asaf Ali

[281] Garnett, D: *The Golden Echo*, publ. by Harcourt, Brace and Company, New York: 1954

[282] http://savarkar.org/en/encyc/2017/5/22/David-Garnett-on-Savarkar.html, accessed 21 April 2019

[283] Srivastava, H

[284] Fischer-Tiné, H

[285] Bandhu, V: *Life and Times of Madan Lal Dhingra*, publ. by Ocean Books, New Delhi: 2013

[286] Yajnik, I

[287] Gandhi, MK (ed. Parel, AJ): *Hind Swaraj and other writings*, publ. by Cambridge University Press: Cambridge: 2009

[288] https://www.inc.in/en/inc-sessions, accessed 7 April 2019

[289] Yajnik, I

[290] Tilak quoted by Yajnik, I

[291] Yajnik, I

[292] https://www.academia.edu/6931584/Zachariah_A_long_strange_trip_the_lives_in_exile_of_Har_Dayal, accessed 7 April 2019

[293] Srivastava, H

[294] Yajnik, I

[295] Number 68 according to: http://www.open.ac.uk/researchprojects/makingbritain/taxonomy/term/566; No. 78 according to http://satyashodh.com/iol1.htm. Both sites accessed 7 April 2019

[296] Joglekar, JD

[297] Congreve, R

[298] Celebrations as described in Srivastava, H

[299] Chand, F: *Lajpat Rai. Life and Work*, publ. by Publications Division, Ministry of Education & Broadcasting: New Delhi: 2010

[300] https://api.parliament.uk/historic-hansard/commons/1907/jun/18/the-unrest-in-india-cases-of-lala-lajpat , accessed 8 April 2019

8

[301] Chand, F

[302] Yajnik, I

[303] The *Punjabee* was a newspaper in India with which Rai was closely connected

[304] Quoted by Yajnik, I

[305] Yajnik, I

[306] Bose, AC

[307] Sardar Ajit Singh (1881–1947) Punjabi nationalist and uncle of Bhagat Singh

[308] https://en.wikipedia.org/wiki/John_Rees_(civil_servant), accessed 12 June 2019

[309] https://api.parliament.uk/historic-hansard/commons/1907/jul/30/seditious-indian-newspapers, accessed 8 April 2019

[310] Rees, JD: *India; the Real India*, publ. by JB Millett Company, Boston: 1910

[311] Times of London: 19 June 1907

[312] Yajnik, I

[313] Yajnik, I

[314] Both quotes from Yajnik, I

[315] Srivastava, H

[316] Bose, AC

[317] Keer, D

[318] Workers: *Some Revolutionary Workers*, http://savarkar.org/en/encyc/2017/5/22/2_03_45_30_SOME_REVO_WORKERS.pdf_1.pdf (pdf file downloaded April 2019)

[319] Details of aims of Abhinav Bharat from Srivastava, H

[320] Srivastava, H

[321] Savarkar quoted in Keer, D

[322] *Times* (London) 19 June 1907

[323] 1857-1954 (https://en.wikipedia.org/wiki/M._P._T._Acharya#India_House, accessed 9 April 2019)

[324] Acharya quoted in Keer, D

[325] Srivastava, H

[326] Srivastava, H

[327] Details of bomb-making story from Srivastava, H

[328] Bhandu, V: *The Life and times of Madan Lal Dhingra*, publ. by Ocean Books, New Delhi: 2013

[329] Bhandu, V

[330] Miss Amaya, a Russian medical doctor studying in Berlin; see: Srivastava, H

[331] Bose, AC

[332] Srivastava, H

[333] https://www.thehindubusinessline.com/blink/explore/saint-in-the-tigers-shadow/article8819953.ece, accessed 10 April 2019

[334] Joglekar, JD

[335] https://en.wikipedia.org/wiki/International_Socialist_Congress,_Stuttgart_1907, accessed 9 April 2019

[336] https://www.marxists.org/archive/lenin/works/1907/oct/00.htm, accessed 9 April 2019

[337] Yajnik, I

[338] Sethna, KA: *Madame Bhikaiji Rustom Cama*, publ. by Ministry of Information and Broadcasting, New Delhi: 2013

[339] Quoted in Yajnik, I

[340] Srivastava, H

[341] Sethna, KA & https://www.boloji.com/articles/920/madame-bhikaji-cama, accessed 9 April 2019

[342] Quoted in Sethna, KA

[343] https://www.marxists.org/archive/lenin/works/1907/oct/20.htm, accessed 9 April 2019

[344] Quoted in Sethna

[345] Srivastava, H

[346] Knight, P: *The British Army in Mesopotamia, 1914-1918*, publ. by McFarland, Jefferson (NC): 1970

[347] Majumdar, RC: *Struggle for Freedom*, publ. by Bharatiya Vidya Bhavan, Bombay: 1988

[348] Anon (Baroda): *Sri Aurobindo and Baroda*, publ. by Sri Aurobindo Society, Baroda: 2014

[349] Majumdar, RC

[350] Bandhu, V

[351] http://www.sriaurobindoinstitute.org/saioc/Sri_Aurobindo/alipore_bomb_case, accessed 10 April 2019

[352] *Times* (London), 4 May 1908

[353] http://www.sriaurobindoinstitute.org/saioc/Sri_Aurobindo/alipore_bomb_case, accessed 10 April 2019

[354] *Times* (London), 2 May 1908

[355] Majumdar, RC

[356] Sri Aurobindo: *Tales of Prison Life*, publ. by Sri Aurobindo Ashram Publication Department, Pondicherry: 1974

[357] http://www.sriaurobindoinstitute.org/saioc/Sri_Aurobindo/alipore_bomb_case, accessed 10 April 2019

[358] Ker, JC

[359] Samanta, AK in https://www.academia.edu/14875154/Chapter_II_Aurobindo_and_Revolutionary_Terrorism, accessed 12 April 2019

[360] Wolpert, SA

[361] Sri Aurobindo

[362] For example, see: *Times* (London) 23 June 1908

[363] Srivastava, H

[364] Srivastava, H

[365] Keer, D

[366] Garnett, D

[367] Srivastava, H

[368] *Times* (London) 23 May 1908

[369] Details from Bandhu, V

[370] *Times* (London) 23 May 1908

[371] Quoted in Keer, D

[372] https://hosted.law.wisc.edu/wordpress/sharafi/files/2010/07/Lincolns-Inn-6.0.pdf, accessed 21 May 2019

[373] Probably, JS Master, correspondent of Bombay based *Parsee* newspaper

[374] Bandhu, V

[375] Bose, AC

[376] Details gleaned from Bandhu, V and Srivastava, H

[377] https://www.smithsonianmag.com/history/pass-it-on-the-secret-that-preceded-the-indian-rebellion-of-1857-105066360/, accessed 23 July 2019

[378] From the introduction to an English translation of the book available to download from Savarkar.org

[379] Srivastava, H

[380] From the introduction to an English translation of the book available to download from

Savarkar.org

381 Bandhu, V
382 Bose, AC
383 Wolpert, SA
384 Joglekar, JD
385 Yajnik, I
386 Joglekar, JD
387 Ker, JC
388 Wolpert, SA
389 Sen, SN
390 Keer, D
391 Wolpert, SA
392 Srivastava, H
393 Ker, JC
394 https://www.gracesguide.co.uk/Central_Technical_College, accessed 13 April 2019
395 Bose, AC
396 Srivastava, H
397 Bose, AC
398 *Times* (London) 17 October 1908
399 *Times* (London) 22 October 1908
400 Bandhu, V
401 *Times* (London) 22 December 1908
402 Srivastava, H
403 See: Sen, SN
404 *Times* (London) 22 December 1908
405 Srivastava, H
406 Details from *Times* (London) 30 December 1908 and Keer, D
407 Probably, Gokul Chand Narang (1878-1969), influenced by Arya Samaj: http://hhshribholanathjimemories.blogspot.com/2012/08/sir-gokul-chand.html, accessed 23 May 2019
408 Probably, Gokul Chand Narang (1878-1969), a law student in London before 1911
409 Keer, D
410 Quoted by Keer, D
411 DNB
412 Srivastava, H
413 http://www.russianpresence.org.uk/index.php/history/3032-russians-in-london-lenin.html and https://helenrappaport.com/footnotes/lenin-in-london/ , accessed 14 April, 2019
414 Bhandu, V
415 Singh, P: *Madan Lal Dhingra: an evaluation of his mission*, publ. in *The Punjab Past and Present* - Volume 37 Part 1, Patiala: April 2006
416 DNB online edition, accessed 15 April 2019
417 Singh, P
418 Gilbert, M: *Servant of India*, publ. by Longmans, London: 1966
419 http://pseweb.eu/ydepot/semin/texte0910/CAS2010BRI.pdf, accessed 15 April 2019
420 Singh, P
421 Gilbert, M
422 Singh, P
423 Solomon, RV & Bond, JW: *Indian States: A Biographical, Historical, and Administrative Survey*, publ. by Asian Educational Services, New Delhi: 2006
424 DNB online, accessed 15 April 2019
425 Visram, R

[426] DNB online, accessed 15 April 2019

[427] Bandhu, V

[428] Singh, P

[429] Srivastava, H

[430] Bose, AC

[431] https://www.oldbaileyonline.org/browse.jsp?id=t19090719-55&div=t19090719-55&terms=Dhingra, accessed 17 April 2019

[432] Joglekar, JD

[433] Bose, AC

[434] Srivastava, H

[435] Times (London) 5 February 1909

[436] Quote and other information about the committee from Tickell, A: *Terrorism, Insurgency and Indian-English Literature, 1830-1947*, publ. by Routledge, New York: 2013

[437] Case summarised from *Times* (London) 12 February 1909

[438] Lahiri, S: *Indians in Britain*, publ. by Frank Cass, London: 2000

[439] *Times* (London) 12 February 1909

[440] *Times* (London) 20 February 1909

[441] *Times* (London) 19 March 1909

[442] Yajnik, I

[443] Yajnik, I

[444] *Times* (London) 1 March 1909

[445] Ghokale, DN: http://savarkar.org/en/pdfs/babarao-savarkar-v003.pdf, downloaded March 2019

[446] Srivastava, H

[447] Ghokale, DN

[448] Much information about Kirtikar from Padmanabhan, RA

[449] Srivastava, H

[450] Much information about Tirumalachari from Padmanabhan, RA

[451] *Times* (London) 22 March 1909

[452] *Times* (London) 4 May 1909

[453] Shyamji was referring to Richard Congreve, Herbert Spencer, Edmund Burke and Robert Wallace

[454] *Times* (London) 7 May 1909

[455] *Times* (London) 7 May 1909

[456] Srivastava, H

[457] Srivastava, H

[458] Bose, AC

[459] Bandhu, V

[460] Singh, P

[461] Singh, P

[462] *Times* (London) 5 July 1909

[463] *Times* (London) 10 June 1909

[464] Yajnik, I

[465] *Times* (London) 6 July 1909

[466] https://www.british-history.ac.uk/survey-london/vol38/pp220-227, accessed 20 April 2019

[467] *Times* (London) 3 July 1909

[468] The description of the murder, the events leading up to it, the quotes, and the trial are abstracted from: Old Bailey Proceedings Online (www.oldbaileyonline.org, version 8.0, 20 April 2019), July 1909, trial of DHINGRA, Madar Lal (25, student) (t19090719-55), accessed in April 2019

12

[469] Quotes from Gilbert, M

[470] Herman, A: *Gandhi and Churchill*, publ. by Random House, New York: 2008

[471] Old Bailey Proceedings Online (www.oldbaileyonline.org, version 8.0, 20 April 2019), July 1909, trial of HORSLEY, Arthur Fletcher (printer), (t19090719-54), accessed 20 April 2019

[472] *Times* (London) 18 August 1909

[473] Srivastava, H

[474] Details of meeting from Padmanabhan, RA

[475] Padmanabhan, RA

[476] Padmanabhan, RA

[477] Bandhu, V

[478] Bandhu, V and http://savarkar.org/en/encyc/2017/5/28/Associates-in-Armed-Revolution.html#/md, accessed 20 April 2019

[479] Padmanabhan, RA

[480] Bose, AC

[481] Srivastava, H

[482] Srivastava, H

[483] Srivastava, H

[484] DNB online, accessed 21 April 2019

[485] https://www.hindujagruti.org/articles/46_madan-lal-dhingra.html, accessed 21 April 2019

[486] Much detail from *Times* (London) 6 July 1909

[487] Bandhu, V

[488] Srivastava, H

[489] Edward Palmer was of mixed Indian and British descent. Maybe, it was he who founded Veeraswamy's Restaurant in London in the 1920s (see: https://erenow.net/biographies/white-mughals-love-and-betrayal-in-eighteenth-century-india/1.php, and https://www.historic-uk.com/CultureUK/The-British-Curry/, both accessed 15 June 2019)

[490] *Times* (London) 8 July 1909

[491] Srivastava, H

[492] Keer, D

[493] *Times* (London) 9 July 1909

[494] *Times* (London) 8 July 1909

[495] Joglekar, JD

[496] Bandhu, V

[497] Private communication from PM Urbach

[498] Shankar, PR: in Proceedings of the Indian History Congress, Vol. 68, Part One (2007), pp. 760-771

[499] *Times* (London) 29 Jan 1909

[500] *Times* (London) 19 June 1909

[501] *Times* (London) 5 July 1909

[502] *Times* (London) 17 July 1909

[503] Srivastava, H

[504] Report of meeting in Bose, AC

[505] Garnett, D

[506] Ker, JC

[507] Joglekar, JD

[508] Garnett, D

[509] e.g.: Bandhu, V and http://savarkar.org/en/encyc/2017/5/28/Associates-in-Armed-Revolution.html#/md, accessed 21 April 2019

[510] This version from: http://savarkar.org/en/encyc/2017/5/28/Associates-in-Armed-Revolution.html#/md, accessed 22 April 2019

[511] Bose, AC

[512] Bose, AC

[513] Hunt, JD

[514] *Indian Opinion* 14 August 1909

[515] 'bhang': a cannabis preparation

[516] Srivastava, H

[517] Hunt, JD

[518] Srivastava, H

[519] Hunt, JD

[520] Parel, AJ (ed.): *Hind Swaraj and Other Writings*, publ. by Cambridge University Press, Cambridge: 2010

[521] Keer, D

[522] Srivastava, H

[523] Fischer-Tiné, H

[524] *Times* (London) 14 February 1910

[525] Quoted in Keer, D

[526] Ker, JC

[527] *Times* (London) 23 December 1909

[528] Ker, JC

[529] *Times* (London) 17 November 1909

[530] Yagnik, I

[531] Yagnik, I

[532] *Times* (London) 7 January 1910

[533] Ker, JC and Bandhu, V

[534] Srivastava, H

[535] Padmanabhan, RA

[536] Srivastava, H

[537] Joglekar, JD

[538] Keer, D

[539] The Act: https://media.sclqld.org.au/documents/digitisation/v03_pp812-827_Criminal%20Law_Fugitive%20Offenders%20Act,%201881%20and%201915.pdf, accessed 23 April 2019

[540] Keer, D

[541] Yagnik, I

[542] Srivastava, H

[543] Padmanabhan, RA

[544] Padmanabhan, RA

[545] Keer, D

[546] Details of Bow Street case from *Times* (London) 15 March 1910

[547] Padmanabhan, RA

[548] Garnett, D

[549] Garnett, D

[550] *Times* (London) 25 April 1910

[551] Sherwood, M: *Origins of Pan-Africanism: Henry Sylvester Williams, Africa, and the African Diaspora*, publ. by Routledge, New York: 2011

[552] *Times* (London) 4 March 1909

[553] *Times* (London) 5 July 1909

[554] *Times* (London) 6 July 1909

[555] Ahmed, F

14

[556] Both quotes from Padmanabhan, RA

[557] Ker, JC

[558] Padmanabhan, RA

[559] *Times* (London) 25 May 1910

[560] *Times* (London) 3 June 1910

[561] *Times* (London)4 June 1910

[562] *Times* (London) 18 June 1910

[563] Padmanabhan, RA

[564] http://brahminsforsociety.com/tamil/2016/06/27/v-v-s-Aiyar-1881-1925/ , accessed 9 July 2019

[565] Srivastava, H

[566] Padmanabhan, RA

[567] Srivastava, H

[568] *Times* (London) 20 July 1910

[569] Keer, D

[570] Srivastava, H

[571] Yagnik, I

[572] Yagnik, I

[573] Keer, D

[574] Keer, D

[575] Srivastava, H

[576] Yagnik, I

[577] Padmanabhan, RA

[578] Quoted in Yagnik, I

[579] Yagnik, I

[580] http://savarkar.org/en/pdfs/L_Humanite_translation.pdf, accessed 27 April 2019

[581] http://savarkar.org/en/pdfs/L_Humanite_translation.pdf, accessed 27 April 2019

[582] https://www.marxists.org/archive/longuet-jean/index.htm, accessed 27 April 2019

[583] Translated in: http://anurupacinar.net/wp-content/uploads/2013/09/Jean-Longuet-translation.pdf, accessed 27 April 2019

[584] *Times* (London) 25 February 1911

[585] Quoted in *Times* (London) 27 February 1911

[586] Keer, D

[587] *Times* (London) 16 September 1910

[588] *Times* (London)16 January 1911

[589] *Times* (London) 27 September 1910

[590] *Times* (London)16 January 1911

[591] Keer, D

[592] Joglekar, JD

[593] Some editions of this are titled *Hindutva. Who is a Hindu?* To read the text, see: Savarkar, VD: *Essentials of Hindutva*, downloaded from Savarkar.org

[594] Hindutva has had a considerable influence on politics in modern India: For example, see: Jaffrelot, C ; Kuruvachira, J; Sharma, J.; and Singh, R., all listed in the bibliography.

[595] Yagnik, I

[596] Joshi, VC

[597] Joshi, VC

[598] Quoted in Varma, GL

[599] https://en.wikipedia.org/wiki/William_Howard_Taft#Europe, accessed 28 April 2019

[600] Varma, GL

[601] *Times* (London) 19 March 1909

[602] Garnett, D

[603] Fischer-Tiné, H

[604] Yagnik, I

[605] Fischer-Tiné, H

[606] Bose, AC

[607] Yagnik, I

[608] Yagnik, I

[609] Yagnik, I

[610] Fischer-Tiné, H

[611] Yagnik, I

[612] Varma, GL

[613] Varma, GL

[614] Yagnik, I

[615] Fischer-Tiné, H

[616] Quoted by Fischer-Tiné, H

[617] Fischer-Tiné, H

[618] Fischer-Tiné, H

[619] Yagnik, I

[620] Quoted by Yagnik, I

[621] Varma, GL

[622] Yagnik, I

[623] Varma, GL

[624] Yagnik, I

[625] Nehru, J: *An Autobiography* (first publ. 1936), reprint publ. by OUP, New Delhi: 1982

[626] Varma, GL

[627] https://ofbjpuk.org/?p=803, accessed 28 April 2019

[628] Yagnik, I

[629] Yagnik, I

[630] Fenner Brockway, A: *The Indian Crisis*, publ. by Victor Gollancz, London: 1930

[631] http://ramchandraj.tripod.com/london_india.txt, accessed 22 May 2019

[632] http://www.hvk.org/2003/0303/121.html, accessed 22 May 2019

[633] i.e.: 'Hindu Freedom Fighter Memorial Institute. I salute you, Mother'

[634] https://www.mkgandhi.org/law_lawyers/appendix7.htm, accessed 17 May 2019

[635] *Times* (London) 7 November 1988

[636] https://www.theguardian.com/uk-news/2015/nov/11/indian-lawyer-disbarred-from-inner-temple-one-century-ago-reinstated, accessed 17 May 2019

[637] https://www.narendramodi.in/cm-pays-tributes-to-shri-shyamji-krishna-varma-5603, accessed 17 May 2019

[638] https://www.krantiteerth.org/viranjali-yatra.html, accessed 17 May 2019

[639] '*viranjal*i' is a word that combines '*vir*' (a valorous person) and '*anjali*' (offering or tribute)

[640] https://www.krantiteerth.org/viranjali-yatra.html, accessed 17 May 2019

[641] Bandhu, V

[642] https://www.indiatoday.in/magazine/indiascope/story/19770115-ashes-of-madan-lal-dhingra-flown-back-to-india-67-years-after-his-death-in-london-823532-2014-07-10, accessed 23 May 2019

[643] https://discovery.nationalarchives.gov.uk/details/r/C11188820, accessed 25 June 2019

[644] https://www.krantiteerth.org/the-making-of-memorial.html, accessed 18 May 2019

[645] i.e: 'Shrine of revolution'

[646] https://www.narendramodi.in/ur/honble-cm-dedicates-kranti-teerth-as-a-memorial-to-shyamji-krishna-verma-3763, accessed 18 May 2019

[647] *Times* (London) 18 December 2010

Printed in Great Britain
by Amazon

74627765R00097